GREEN WOOD
Turning

GREEN WOOD
Turning

**EXPERT TECHNIQUES, HANDY TIPS
& 10 SKILL-BUILDING PROJECTS**

CHRISTIAN ZEPPETZAUER

Other Schiffer Books on Related Subjects:

Spalted Wood: The History, Science, and Art of a Unique Material, Sara C. Robinson, Hans Michaelsen, and Julia C. Robinson, ISBN 978-0-7643-5038-2

Turning Bowls, Dick Sing, ISBN 978-0-7643-1795-8

Multi-Axis Spindle Turning: A Systematic Exploration, Barbara Dill, ISBN 978-0-7643-5534-9

Copyright © 2025 by Schiffer Publishing, Ltd.

Originally published as *Grünholz-deschseln für Einsteiger*, by Leopold Stocker Verlag GmbH, Graz © 2015.
Translated from the German by Rachel Joerges

Library of Congress Control Number: 2024952381

All rights reserved. No part of this work may be reproduced or used in any form or by any means—graphic, electronic, or mechanical, including photocopying or information storage and retrieval systems—without written permission from the publisher.

The scanning, uploading, and distribution of this book or any part thereof via the Internet or any other means without the permission of the publisher is illegal and punishable by law. Please purchase only authorized editions and do not participate in or encourage the electronic piracy of copyrighted materials.

"Schiffer Craft" and the crane logo are registered trademarks of Schiffer Publishing, Ltd.

Interior design by: Lori Malkin Ehrlich
Cover design by: Lindsay Hess
Edited by: Kaylee Schofield
Technical consultation by: Luke Voytas
Type set in DIN 2014 Demi and DIN 2014 Light

ISBN: 978-0-7643-6963-6
ePub: 978-1-5073-0625-3

The following images are credited to their respective creators via Shutterstock.com: page 19 apple wood: bieszczady_wildlife.

Printed in China

Published by Schiffer Craft
An imprint of Schiffer Publishing, Ltd.
4880 Lower Valley Road
Atglen, PA 19310
Phone: (610) 593-1777; Fax: (610) 593-2002
Email: info@schifferbooks.com
Web: www.schifferbooks.com

For our complete selection of fine books on this and related subjects, please visit our website at www.schifferbooks.com. You may also write for a free catalog.

Schiffer Publishing's titles are available at special discounts for bulk purchases for sales promotions or premiums. Special editions, including personalized covers, corporate imprints, and excerpts, can be created in large quantities for special needs. For more information, contact the publisher.

We are always looking for people to write books on new and related subjects.
If you have an idea for a book, please contact us at proposals@schifferbooks.com.

Contents

Preface 9

Introduction 12

Wood as a Living Resource 14
Wood Growth 14
Shrinkage and Swelling 16
Wood Glossary 18
    Maple 18
    Apple. 19
    Pear 19
    Boxwood. 19
    Yew 20
    Alder. 20
    Cherry 20
    Walnut 21
    Olive 21
    Beech 21
    Hornbeam 22
    Pine. 22
    Plum 22

Storing and Keeping Green Wood 23
Storage Options 23
Drying Workpieces 25

Wood Characteristics 26

Growth Factors 27

  Crookedness 27

  Forked Growth 29

  Eccentric Growth 29

  Tree Taper 30

  Asymmetrical Trunks, Hollows, and Strong Root Growth 31

Structural Factors 32

  Irregular Growth Ring Structure 32

  Rippled Growth 32

  Burls 33

  Reaction Wood 34

  Twisted Growth 35

  Resin Pockets 36

  Branchiness... 36

  Abnormal Heartwood Formation 38

Factors Due to External Influences 38

  Cracks 38

    Shrinkage Cracks 38

    Frost Cracks 39

    Dry Cracks and Heat Cracks 39

    Heartwood Cracks 39

  Ring Shakes 39

Man-Made Damage 40

  Ingrown Foreign Objects 41

  Felling Damage 41

  Incorrect Felling Times 42

  Transport Damage.. 42

  Environmental Factors 42

Wildlife Damage.. 43

  Damage Due to Game Browsing 43

  Damage by Wood-Destroying Insects..................... 43

    Common Furniture Beetle 44

    Greater Horntail 44

    Carpenter Ant 44

    Bark Beetle 45

Wood Diseases... 46

  Wood-Destroying Fungi.................................... 47

    Brown Rot 47

    White Rot 47

    Simultaneous Decomposition 47

  Wood-Discoloring Fungi 47

    Blue Fungus 47

Sourcing Green Wood 48

Projects 50
Small Turned Tree. 51
Long-Stemmed Cup 57
Flower Vase 75
Lidded Vessel 82
Ball 95
Bark Bowl 107
Bark Bowl Variation 115
Natural Plum Wood Bowl 122
Natural Applewood Bowl 128
Plate 132

Sharpening Turning Tools 140
What Affects Sharpness? 141
Power Sharpening 141
    Sharpening Woodturning Chisels 145
    Sharpening Finishing Tools 146
    Sharpening Turning Gouges. 146
Hand Sharpening 148

Surface Finishing 151
Stains 152
Varnishes 153
Oils and Waxes. 153

Inspiration Gallery 156

Postscript 158

Appendix 159
Glossary. 159
References 159
Additional Resources 159
Index. 160

Preface

**Where would our trade be without wood—
this wonderful raw material from the forest?**

Few living beings on Earth are larger or more impressive than the numerous tree species that shape large parts of each continent. Almost a third of Germany and Switzerland and almost half of Austria are covered by forest. The gifts that forests provide are extraordinarily diverse. Not only do they form an important part of our cultural landscape, but they also provide an important living and recreational space for us humans and supply us with berries, mushrooms, game, and, last but not least, wood. Healthy forests also offer us protection from natural hazards and contribute significantly to the quality of our air and water.

A natural forest is also a habitat rich in different species. The composition of species can change from day to day over the course of a year. The tree layer, shrub layer, and herb layer offer sunny and shady, dry and moist, and nutrient-rich and nutrient-poor areas. Young plants thrive alongside old and dead wood. These different conditions make it possible for a variety of organisms to exist alongside one another.

A beautiful bowl made from plum wood.

A natural forest is a habitat rich with different species.

A long walk through the forest with open eyes shows us the astonishing diversity, the wealth of species, and the beauty of this unique habitat, which is far too often taken for granted. Many of nature's moods make the woodturner's heart beat faster—guided by creativity and imagination, they can already see the finished turned project. What would humans be without the forest?

I would like to dedicate this book to those who are exploring green woodworking for the first time and want to discover this new ground step by step. Increasing craftsmanship skills is possible only step by step, from the bottom up. One's first expe-

If you walk through the forest with your eyes open, you will certainly find material for your projects.

We should also be aware that the creatures in the forest (birds, bees, beetles, insects, game, etc.) are far more numerous than humans, need this habitat to survive, and therefore have a greater claim to it. The forest reacts sensitively to changes and is always trying to correct external influences. It is therefore all the more important to treat forests with care and respect. Raising awareness should begin at an early age, since it is not just mankind that the forest is irreplaceable for.

riences in turning green wood should be done in the context of the simplest projects.

It was important for me to design the projects in such a way that each person can choose their own difficulty level by freely selecting the material thickness. The thinner the workpieces are turned, the greater the difficulty of the work steps you need to master. In this way, every woodturner can gradually and slowly improve their skills. I have deliberately avoided using many of the specialized tools used in green woodturning and will not mention them in this book, **focusing primarily on the basic tools and techniques a person should know.** The numerous photos, which took great effort to produce, are intended to illustrate the individual work steps and supplement the text. It is also important to me to go into some of the wood's characteristics and flaws. However, in this context I would like to avoid creating a highly scientific book, so the scope will remain limited to the essentials.

—Christian Zeppetzauer, BEd

Introduction

Green woodturning is neither a modern trend nor a newly invented technique. Even my great-grandfather turned bowls, plates, and dishes from green wood to shorten their drying time. The bowls were turned from green wood with an allowance of at least ¾" (1.9 cm) so that they could then be gently dried. The workpieces were stored in the hay barn, where they were covered with hay and dried within a few weeks, depending on the size, type of wood, and moisture content. These bowls, which had become slightly deformed due to the shrinkage of the wood, were then turned once again and given their final shape. The deformed, oval appearance of the bowl was less desirable back then than it is today. At that time, people made mainly utilitarian objects.

A simple bowl turned from fresh wood.

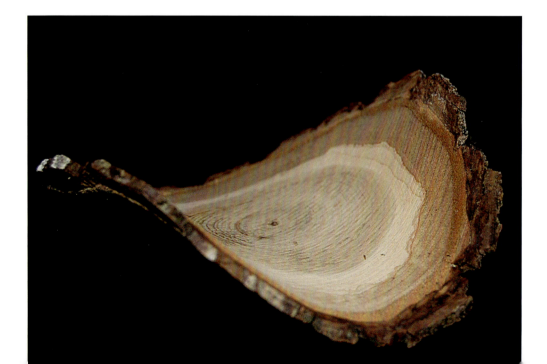

Many a pile of green wood offers real treasures.

In this country setting, the design was considered secondary to the function, and, unlike today, there was no time to experiment. Nowadays, more and more artistically designed collector's items are being created.

The main difference between green woodturning and conventional woodturning is that there is complete freedom of form. You do not have to adhere to dimensional specifications, nor do any two pieces have to look the same. While wood flaws, which I prefer to call "characteristics," are partially or completely undesirable in conventional woodturning, it is often precisely these characteristics that give a green wood object a special touch. It is these random features that make working with green wood so interesting. The freedom to decide on the shape of a piece while working on it or to change it spontaneously is also a completely new experience when turning. When you're turning green wood, the idea that a careless mistake while turning can result in a huge amount of extra work is partially or completely eliminated. Green woodturning opens possibilities for shaping and material thicknesses that would never be possible with dry wood.

The ease with which shavings can be removed from green wood is due to the light texture and malleability of its structure. The otherwise noticeable differences between hard and soft annual rings are hardly recognizable. Rapid material removal is possible with special tools and the ability to remove large amounts of shavings at once. In contrast, green wood-turning also makes it possible to create objects with wafer-thin material thicknesses that would never be possible with dry wood.

In general, green wood is easier to obtain and store than dry wood. The green wood-turner can find real treasures in many a brush pile. Turning green wood is not everyone's cup of tea, but the same applies to conventional or commercial woodturning. I know a lot of people who only wanted to try working with green wood but became so enthusiastic about it that they now almost exclusively turn green wood.

Green wood or not—the most important thing is that the work is fun and you can enjoy what you have created.

Very creative bowls can be made from unusual wood.

INTRODUCTION

Wood Growth

Shrinkage and Swelling

Wood Glossary

Wood as a Living Resource

Next to stone, wood is the oldest material used in construction. Since man began to use wood for countless purposes, many other materials have been discovered and developed. But none of them have replaced good old wood. On the contrary, it is just as popular today as it was a thousand years ago. Wood is irreplaceable and indispensable at the same time.

Alongside horn, ivory, resin, and plastic, wood is the turner's most important material. In contrast to carpenters, who work mainly with the trunk of a tree, woodturners also use roots, rootstocks, burls, and branches. Wood is a fantastic material, but also an unpredictable one. To make work easier and avoid disappointment, you should know the basic properties of this fundamental material.

Wood Growth

The absorption of nutrient salts from the soil and carbon dioxide (CO_2) from the air produces glucose and starch or cellulose. This transformation, which is the growth of the tree, is called assimilation. In our latitudes, tree growth begins in spring and lasts until late summer and fall. During the winter months, trees grow more slowly.

Length growth begins with the sprouting of the terminal or shoot buds of the trunk, branches, and twigs. As the terminal buds strive for sunlight, tall trunks grow in dense tree populations, while half or short trunks develop in more-exposed tree populations.

Trunk Structure

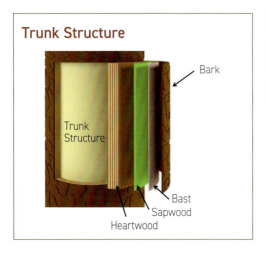

Thickness growth takes place in the cambium. The cambium is a thin layer of cells that surrounds the wooden parts of the tree like a cylinder. Due to the continuous cell division in the cambium, ring-like growth zones are formed on the tree trunk, which make up the annual growth rings.

Because cell division is faster in the spring than in the summer and fall, two different growth zones are formed in hardwoods and softwoods each year. The cells formed in spring are thinner walled, lighter, and softer than those formed in fall, which are darker and harder. From a functional point of view, water-conducting tissue is formed in the spring and strengthening tissue in the summer. Together, they form an annual ring. Growth slows down toward the end of the year.

Generally, trees only ever use the younger, outer areas of the trunk to transport and store water. This wood is known as sapwood and is the tree's water supply from the root to the crown.

The presence of starch in the cells makes it more susceptible to fungal attack and wood-destroying insects. Sapwood is therefore living, active wood in a standing tree. After a few years, the cells cease to function. Most tree species then store organic and inorganic substances such as tannins and orthosilicic acid in these cells and seal them. This wood inside the trunk is called heartwood.

The sapwood in trees is responsible for transporting water from the roots to the crown.

The annual rings are formed each year by two different growth zones.

WOOD GROWTH

Although the heartwood is no longer active, it offers support to the tree. Due to the stored substances, this wood is darker in color and more resistant to fungal and insect infestation. Heartwood also absorbs less water when moistened. This wood is therefore very difficult to soak.

Shrinkage and Swelling

A living tree stores a lot of water in its wood. For example, 35 cubic feet (1m³) of freshly cut spruce wood can contain up to 80 gallons (300 liters). This is stored in the cellular wall and cavities. In a living tree, the water content is generally not evenly distributed in the trunk cross section. As already mentioned, there is always a particularly high water content in the sapwood. In addition, the tree tries to fill at least 90%–95% of the pore space in the outer sapwood with water as a defense against fungal spores and insects. In the inner part of the trunk—the heartwood, which is not as important for the tree's vital functions—the wood moisture content is lower. For softwoods, it is around 40%. Wood's moisture content can change, thus changing its weight and dimensions (swelling, shrinkage) through the absorption or release of moisture.

Three different shrinkage measurements of wood: length, diameter, and circumference.

Shrinkage varies depending on the type of wood, density, and grain direction in the tree trunk.

The water in the cell cavities is referred to as free water, whereas the water in the cell walls is defined as bound water. When you are drying wood from freshly fallen trees, the "free" water is first released from the cell cavities. Only when the free water has been removed is the "bound" water extracted from the cell wall. The junction between the removal of free and bound water is called the fiber saturation point, which is around 30%. From the point at which the water is removed from the cell walls, the wood begins to shrink. This leads to a change in volume, resulting in deformation and cracking.

At a certain temperature and relative humidity, the wood tends to adopt a very specific moisture content. This causes the wood to dry. Moisture equilibrium is ultimately achieved when no more moisture can be released from the wood to the surrounding area or absorbed from it.

Wood typically shrinks and swells perpendicular to the grain. It has three different shrinkage rates, which in the case of freshly cut wood are 0.1%–0.5% in length, 3%–6% in diameter, and 6%–12% in circumference. The amount of shrinkage largely depends on the type of wood, hardness, density, grain direction in the trunk, and difference in moisture content.

Shrinkage cracks caused by internal tension.

The shrinkage in millimeters of a board with a width of 15¾" (400 mm) can be calculated as follows. An internal moisture content of 25% and a final moisture content of 12% are assumed.

Tangential shrinkage = 7%
Difference in wood moisture = 25% minus 12% = 13%

Difference in shrinkage = $\frac{7 \times 13}{3}$ equals 3.0%

Shrinkage = $\frac{400 \times 3.0}{100}$ equals 12 mm

The board shrinks 7/16" (11.1 mm) in width.

SHRINKAGE AND SWELLING

Heartwood boards and posts become thinner toward the bark because sapwood shrinks more than heartwood.

Buckling of side boards caused by shrinkage.

Heartwood planks and posts have vertical growth rings. This is why this sawn timber becomes thinner toward the bark, because the sapwood shrinks more than the heartwood. This is also the reason for the buckling in side boards, where the right side (the side facing the heartwood) rounds and the left side becomes hollow.

A large moisture differential can lead to uneven shrinkage in radial and tangential directions. This causes internal stresses in the wood and subsequent shrinkage cracks. These cracks are smaller in timber that doesn't contain pith than in sawn timber containing pith. The lower the mass present, the lower the cracking and the higher the warpage.

The following therefore applies to green woodturning: **the thinner an object, the less cracking there is**, since the tension inside the wood can be released. This results in deformation due to the different shrinkage dimensions. In principle, however, turned objects made from green wood should be dried gently.

Wood Glossary

Maple

Maple comes in several varieties, including hard maple and Norway maple. Hard maple can vary from ivory to reddish or light brown in tone, whereas Norway maple is tinted slightly yellow to slightly gray. Maple wood shows a clear yellowing with age. The sapwood of maple does not differ in color from the heartwood.

Apple

The apple tree is found on all continents in both cultivated and wild species. Applewood is pink to reddish brown, often with darker stripes and irregular, flat, dark areas, making this wood very decorative. The pride of many an old carpenter was a self-made applewood woodworking plane that was carefully cared for over many years for this purpose.

Pear

Pear wood has a fairly uniform appearance—the color ranges from pale gray to reddish brown. Older trunks are often intensely red and darken strongly to a brownish color. Pear wood is usually steamed to even out and deepen the reddish color.

Boxwood

The shrub-like growing trunks only very rarely reach maximum dimensions of 10–13 feet (3–4 m) in length and a diameter of $11^{13}/_{16}$" (30 cm). Boxwood is yellowish with a brownish or greenish tinge, often with faint dark stripes. Boxwood is very susceptible to discoloration caused by moisture and fungi.

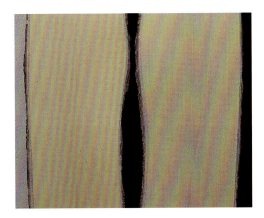

WOOD GLOSSARY

Yew

Yew wood has strikingly narrow, mostly wavy growth rings with narrow, dark late wood without resin channels. The wood is yellowish to reddish brown, usually with a violet tinge, although this characteristic is lost as the wood darkens. In Austria and Germany the yew is a protected species, and there are only a few counted specimens of this slow-growing tree, which can live to be over two thousand years old. The little wood that is commercially available is imported. The wood of the yew was valued in prehistoric times for weapons and tools, and Ice Age hunters used yew spears for hunting mammoths, as well-preserved discoveries have clearly demonstrated.

Alder

Black, white, and gray alder are widespread in Europe and can also be found throughout the western United States. The wood of the white or gray alder is less valuable: it is lighter and inferior in quality to black alder. The heartwood and sapwood do not differ in color. Their color ranges from yellow to orange, which darkens to brownish.

Cherry

This tree can be found in cultivated and wild species in all parts of the world. The color of the wood is pale yellow to red, occasionally greenish and green striped. The cherry tree tends to darken to an orange-reddish brown. It requires careful care as trunk wood and as sawn timber to avoid unsightly discoloration. The wood of the wild cherry is finer in structure, finer grained, and of a beautifully even color. The cultivated cherry, on the other hand, is usually coarser, has wider and uneven growth rings, and is of a different yellowish color.

Walnut

The walnut tree is found in the United States and Europe, but also in Asia Minor, northern India, and China. This tree is characterized by its rich, dark brown color and slight iridescence when sanded to a fine grit.

Olive

Olive wood is yellowish brown with striking, irregular stripes of different widths on all kinds of cuts and cohesive spot formations, resulting in beautiful, lively, and often-distinctive marbled patterns.

Beech

The American beech can be found throughout the eastern United States and into southern Canada, whereas the European beech is found throughout Europe. This plant's heartwood and sapwood do not differ in color. The color is whitish gray with a pale yellowish to reddish tinge. It is very versatile and is one of the most commonly used timbers (plywood, furniture, flooring, etc.). Beechwood has high shrinkage and is hard, firm, and easy to work with. Steaming beechwood evens out and intensifies its reddish color and improves its durability.

WOOD GLOSSARY

Hornbeam

The hornbeam is found in different parts of Europe. The color of the wood is yellowish white to slightly light gray. Heartwood and sapwood do not differ in color. One of the special characteristics of hornbeam is its toughness and high wear resistance.

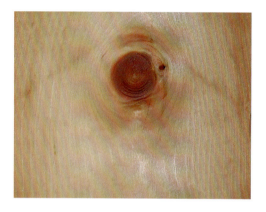

Pine

Pine (including eastern white pine and ponderosa pine) is an affordable and easily accessible material for North American woodturners. For those based in Europe, Swiss stone pine is popular. The stone pine grows in the high mountains and can grow up to 82 feet (25 m) high in favorable locations and can reach a diameter of up to 31" (approx. 80 cm). The pith of this wood is light reddish, while the sapwood is yellowish to white. Swiss stone pine is very soft and light and shrinks very little. Whether you're working with North American pine or Swiss stone pine, this fragrant wood should be deresinated before finishing.

Plum

Plum wood is hard, dense, and somewhat brittle. The color ranges from red to violet brown with light and dark stripes. A striking feature is the intense purple tint in places, although this fades over time. The small dimensions limit the processing options for this very decorative wood.

Storing and Keeping Green Wood

Storage Options

Drying Workpieces

In contrast to conventional wood storage (the aim of which is drying), when you're storing green wood, the drying process should be delayed for as long as possible. However, depending on the type of wood, this type of specialized storage is possible for only a limited time.

Storage Options

It is advisable to store green wood in damp, shady places that are protected from drafts. Take special care to avoid fungal and insect infestation. Wood species such as beech and maple are particularly at risk. If there is a surface fungal infestation, the bark must be removed to prevent the wood from becoming infected (continuous fungal infestation). However, this has the disadvantage that the removed bark causes the wood to dry out more quickly. Also, the end-grain areas of a piece of wood release a lot of moisture very quickly, which means that the risk of cracking is particularly high. However, this can be counteracted with minimal effort. Coating with glue is a measure widely used for this. Another option for storing green wood is **submerging it in water**. The wood dimensions will dictate the size and type of container you use.

Barrels or water troughs are well suited for this. With this type of storage, the water must be replaced regularly, first to prevent the formation of algae and second to prevent the fermentation process that would otherwise occur. During the fermentation process, the starch present in the wood is converted into

STORAGE OPTIONS

Storage in water.

fructose, which subsequently causes a foul-smelling odor. You can use this method to store green wood for several months.

Pieces of wood can also be temporarily stored by using the **moisture in the soil**. Place the piece of the tree in a shady, cool place, with the cut side facedown on the ground. This prevents the end grain from drying out too quickly, since it is protected through the moisture in the soil.

You can also wrap the wood with **water-soaked cloths** to prevent it from drying out prematurely. Wrapping green wood with nylon foil can be done only to a limited extent. Since this seal is not 100% airtight, there is a risk of mold growth during prolonged storage. For unfinished work, however, this is a very good way of protecting the project from drying out in the short term. In this way, a few days can be bridged without risk until the project is finished.

Wood stored by using the moisture in the soil.

STORING AND KEEPING GREEN WOOD

Drying Workpieces

Finished turned objects must be dried carefully. Under no circumstances should you dry objects that are at risk of cracking in centrally heated rooms. A cool, well-ventilated room is suitable for the first few days. After that, drying can be carried out more quickly indoors. A good option for gentle drying is to wrap the workpiece in dry wooden shavings.

I will explain the exact process while making a natural-edge bowl from plum wood (see p.122).

There is another type of drying, but it involves the use of chemicals. I will not explore this type of drying here because chemicals, in whatever form, are not harmonious with wood. Every woodworker should get to know the wood, its properties, and the problems associated with it—then gradually learn how to deal with them.

Gently dry the wood by packing it in wood shavings.

Growth Factors

Structural Factors

Factors Due to External Influences

Man-Made Damage

Wildlife Damage

Wood Diseases

A dead branch does not necessarily have to be considered a defect for the green woodturner.

Wood Characteristics

Wood defects are all deviations from the normal condition of the trunk or wood. The growth, development, and internal structure of the wood depend on many external conditions such as the climate, soil conditions, and locale. Some deviations from normal growth can also result in interesting and valuable creative possibilities for the woodturner.

The characteristic wood and bark features also give each tree an unmistakable, individual shape. These characteristics are not automatically to be considered wood defects. Only the point of view determines whether they are a feature or a defect.

These trees are useless for the lumberyard, but not for the green woodturner.

From the tree's point of view, something can be considered a wood defect only if it significantly restricts its life expectancy. Branches, which are indispensable parts of the tree, must not be classified as wood defects. Unique trunk shapes, trunk bulges, and the like are also not a dealbreaker.

From the point of view of the wood user, we speak of wood defects when the intended use is restricted or even made impossible. Mere nuances of form, on the other hand, should not be viewed as flaws but as opportunities. The aesthete welcomes them, enjoying the wood's natural richness and personality. There are **three main groups of wood characteristics**:

- growth factors
- structural factors
- factors due to external influences

Humans can also influence the quality of wood. Environmental influences such as climate, animals, and disease can also contribute to a range of special wood characteristics.

Growth Factors

Whether a wood change or wood characteristic is seen as a defect depends on the intended use. Some wood characteristics can be used as an advantageous feature.

Crookedness

This refers to **a one-sided or two-sided deviation of the trunk axis from the straight line**. A straight trunk is referred to as "two-stranded," a trunk that is bent in one direction is referred to as "one-stranded," and a trunk that bends in several directions is referred to as "unstranded." The term "stranded" comes from

GROWTH FACTORS

the strand of a plumb bob, which hangs from the tree trunk and either comes in contact with the trunk or not.

> **We distinguish among the following:**
> - Two-stranded, straight on both sides (good structural timber)
> - Single-stranded, crooked on one side (large offcuts, wood waste, warped)
> - Unstranded, crooked on both sides (very large offcuts, wood waste, warped)

Many tree species have a genetic predisposition to crookedness or creep. Crookedness can also be caused by unfavorable soil conditions, snow or

One-sided . . .

. . . and two-sided deviation of the trunk.

wind pressure, and other factors. A trunk can also become crooked if the top breaks and a side branch takes over the top shoot's role.

When measuring a tree's level of curvature, do not include the roots, as roots behave differently than trunks. Accompanying wood defects usually include pith displacement, reaction wood, lack of roundness, and an irregular growth ring structure.

To reduce the impact of this feature, I recommend the following:

- Short working lengths
- Placing necessary cross sections in the largest curvature or in the place where curvature changes
- Cutting single-stranded curves horizontally along the arc

Forked Growth

This growth form often occurs due to geological soil conditions (water veins), game browsing, snow pressure, lightning strikes, etc. If two trunk feet grow together during thickness growth and form common annual rings, this is called "false forking." If a tree shaft divides with only one pitch, it is called "true forking." Even if the primary shoot is damaged or destroyed, the side branches take over its function, which leads to forking.

Forking often results in discoloration and areas of rot, as well as false heartwood in beech, bark ingrowth, and twisted grain. However, the interesting double center and the color changes toward the middle of the trunk make a fork very interesting for the turner.

Intertwined forking.

Eccentric Growth

Eccentric growth is when **the pith does not sit exactly in the center of the trunk cross section.** This form of growth usually occurs in combination with red annual rings (reaction wood, compression, or tension wood).

The pith is not located in the center of the trunk cross section.

True forking.

GROWTH FACTORS

This wood is difficult to work with, since it warps dramatically. It can therefore not be used for load-bearing parts and is particularly unfavorable for technical wood drying. This eccentric growth is often caused by one-sided stress due to wind, sun, snow, crown shape, or slope.

Due to its red annual rings, this wood is difficult to work with because it shrinks and twists.

One-sided strain is often the cause of eccentric growth.

Tree Taper

Tree taper is a strong reduction in the trunk diameter. Spruce and fir taper less than pine or many hardwood species. Hornbeam and yew have a strong predisposition to taper. Tree species, age, height, and, above all, location determine the degree of tapering. Trees with neighbors are particularly prone to tapering. Trees without crown competition form an expansive crown, which increases thickness growth as well as stability. The disadvantages are a low timber yield and large waste in the case of rotary-cut and sliced veneers. In addition, the bending strength is reduced when it comes to tapered material, since many of the wood fibers are severed.

Gauging Tapering in a Tree

- Not tapered: diameter changes by up to $3/8$" (1 cm) per linear meter
- Tapered: diameter changes by $3/8$" to $13/16$" (1–2 cm) per linear meter
- Strongly tapered: diameter changes by over $13/16$" (2 cm) per linear meter

Tapering: significant reduction in trunk diameter.

WOOD CHARACTERISTICS

Asymmetrical Trunks, Hollows, and Strong Root Growth

These characteristics belong to the group of irregularities in the outline. **Asymmetrical trunks** are those that have **many irregular indentations and bulges in the cross section**; these indentations also include creases, which affect the bark. They also continue in the wood in the form of wavy annual rings. As a result, the material's utility is greatly reduced and the wood is sometimes unusable. White beech, birch, fir, yew, acacia, and black locusts are prone to asymmetrical trunks. The cause of this is uneven division activity in the cambium, which can be caused by injuries, genetic disposition, or other factors.

The **groove-like indentations** on the trunk that follow the grain are known as **hollows**. These usually begin below the shady branches and extend down to the root collar. They are particularly easy to recognize on smooth-barked trees.

Hollows can be traced back to a lack of trunk parts below these branches. These "starvation branches" need the wood assimilates for their own consumption, so they are not available to assist with the thickness growth of the trunk below the branch base.

Particularly **pronounced trunk feet** are referred to as **strong root growth**. Elm, birch, and bald cypress are particularly affected. For structural reasons, such roots can increase the stability of the trunk on soft ground. Genetic predisposition is also responsible for this wood characteristic.

Hollow caused by a starving branch.

Cross section of an asymmetrical trunk.

GROWTH FACTORS

Structural Factors

Irregular Growth Ring Structure

This is considered a wood defect only if there is a clear change in the width of the annual rings. We distinguish among three different forms:

First, there are **wide annual rings on the inside and narrow annual rings on the outside**. This is the plant's natural structure. As the trees grow larger, the annual ring width decreases because the surrounding trees become an obstruction, hindering quick growth.

The second form is characterized **by narrow growth rings on the inside and wide growth rings on the outside**. This form is particularly noticeable with dense natural regeneration or dense sowing. When the population is reduced, the trees suddenly have more space and light and grow faster. The last form is **changing annual ring widths** due to climatic influences or insect damage. A uniform annual ring structure is often associated with high value and quality. In the case of softwood, narrow annual rings improve the physical properties of the wood, since the proportion of late wood is increased.

In hardwoods, narrow growth rings indicate mild, relatively soft wood. A change in the annual ring width therefore also means a change in the hardness of the wood, which has a negative effect on surface processing. A uniform annual ring structure increases the wood's ability to resonate, which is very important for musical-instrument makers, for example.

The annual ring width is therefore an indication of internal branchiness, density and strength, surface quality after processing, uniformity of wood properties, dimensional stability, and growth processes.

Rippled Growth

Irregular grain growth is a **deviation from the normal grain pattern**. Longitudinal rippled growth (or false rippled growth) refers to tangentially wavy, washboard-like indentations that are visible on the trunk. Longitudinal rippled growth is most frequently found in beech, chestnut, lime, and birch. Transverse rippled growth, also known as true rippled growth, is a finely wavy annual ring pattern that is visible on the cross-sectional surface. The annual rings run in short, wavy lines. Transverse rippled

A change in the width of the annual rings means a change in the hardness of the wood.

True rippled growth seen on the cross-sectional surface.

Rare tangential rippled growth.

growth occurs mainly in spruce and fir trees that grow to greater heights, but also in maple and ash. In softwoods, this characteristic is very popular for musical instruments.

In addition to these rippled growth structures, there are also unique textures (such as flamed). Such wood is difficult to work with but is very popular as veneer wood due to its striking appearance.

Burls

Burl growth can be found on the rootstock due to the many small root growths or overgrowth of bud accumulations and injuries. The wood fibers of the

Cross section of a burl growth.

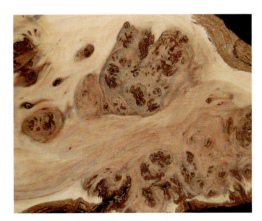
Tuberous burl growth on a trunk.

Root burl growth.

STRUCTURAL FACTORS

annual rings run irregularly and curved in this area. This results in unique, beautiful, and coveted wood structures. Burl veneers, which are used mainly for inlay work, are, however, available only in small dimensions.

It has been observed that trees in parks, cities, and open fields are more likely to form burls and tubers than in wooded areas. These trees are exposed to a greater risk of injury and greater stress (emissions, drought, heat) during their lifetime than others. The risk of infection is also greater in cities and in more-populous areas. Parasites can also penetrate injured areas and stimulate the growth of the formation tissue, whereby the infected regions are increasingly enriched with nutrients and growth hormones. This results in an almost unbridled growth in thickness, which leads to benign or malignant tumors.

Reaction wood also forms on strong branches.

The tree tries to ensure stability by balancing one-sided loads.

Reaction Wood

Due to long-term or permanent one-sided stress on the tree, conifers form compression wood to ensure their stability. These stresses can include wind, snow, slopes, or an asymmetrical crown formation. In the first years of a tree's life, no reaction wood is formed, since the bending strength is still high due to the small cross section.

Compression wood, also known as redwood or boxwood, stands out due to its reddish color and its increased proportion of late wood. There is usually an additional shift of the pith to the side facing the wind. Compression wood also differs from normal wood in its density and strong swelling and shrinking. It also has a higher lignin content. Similar to compression wood in softwoods, **tension wood** forms in hardwoods under particular loads, espe-

Compression folds on the inner side of load-bearing hardwood.

cially in trees that lean. Significant compression folds can form on the insides of these.

Tension wood forms in areas subject to bending tension, has a whitish appearance, and shows no recognizable growth ring structure. It has a higher cellulose content, which can show up in sawn timber as having a woolly appearance. In terms of behavior when it comes to swelling and shrinkage, it behaves similarly to compression wood.

Twisted Growth

Twisted growth is a **spiral deviation of the longitudinal fibers from the straight line**. The wood fibers spiral around the pith. On roundwood, the twist can be seen only on the outer parts of the trunk and on the bark. To a lesser extent, almost all wood exhibits some kind of twisted growth.

Disadvantages are strong distortions (skewing), warping, and jamming of the saw, as well as large differences in swelling and shrinkage behavior. However, the twisted grain of a tree also acts like a rope that wraps around the tree, giving it greater bending strength. The structure shows dark and light stripes. This can be affected by wind, location, soil conditions, water veins, and genetic predisposition.

Twisted growth, recognizable by the spiral-shaped distortion of the longitudinal fibers.

STRUCTURAL FACTORS

Resin Pockets

Resin pockets are tangential cracks in the cambium of resin-bearing conifers caused by wind at the beginning of the growing season, which are filled with resin and remain in the wood. They occur in spruce, Scots pine, larch, and pine, but not in fir. In larch, resin pockets often lead to incomplete heartwood formation (recognizable by the light spots next to the resin pockets). The wood's usability can be considerably reduced by resin pockets, depending on their size and number.

Branches extend from the pith.

A tangential crack filled with resin.

Branchiness

Branches are a natural and necessary part of every tree. They originate from the pith of the trunk, and, as long as the branch is exposed to the sun and is actively involved in the life of the tree, they are firmly attached to the underlying trunk wood.

If a branch dies, the subsequent annual rings surround the dead branch. This branch scar is particularly recognizable in beech trees. The strong elevation of the trunk above an overgrown branch break creates a branch bulge. Each branch basically disturbs the natural wood structure of the trunk. To avoid endangering the stability of the tree, the tree reinforces this area by surrounding the branch with a tighter fiber structure.

A branch encased by a knot.

Enclosed dead branch.

WOOD CHARACTERISTICS

Branch scar.

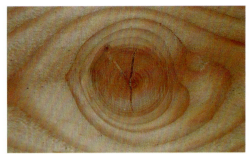

Green branch.

Black branch.

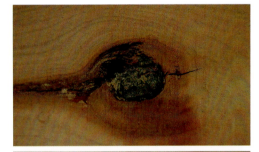

Rotten branch (above) and deeply rotten branch (below).

It's important to distinguish among the following types of branches:

- **Overgrown branches (green branches):** These are healthy branches that still had leaves or needles when they broke off.
- **Dead branches (dry branches, black branches):** They are already dead when they break off or consist only of a branch stump. They are no longer or only partially intergrown and can become dislodged during processing.
- **Rotten branches:** These show obvious signs of decomposition in the branch area.
- **Wing branches:** These reduce bending strength and lead to severe warping. They appear when branches are cut lengthwise.

The utilitarian value of the wood decreases with the increasing number, diameter, and poor condition of the branches. The dry branch zone in particular is a hindrance. Branches disrupt the grain pattern and grain flow, the different densities result in different shrinkage rates, and the strength properties also decrease with increasing branchiness. This is why

STRUCTURAL FACTORS

Wing branch.

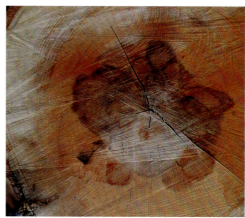

Red heartwood.

branchiness is an important sorting characteristic when you're buying. For the woodturner, these characteristics are aesthetic, natural, and exciting.

Abnormal Heartwood Formation

Abnormal heartwood formation (also known as incorrect heartwood formation, facultative heartwood formation, or false heartwood formation) refers to heartwood formation in wood species that do not normally form a colored heartwood.

In copper beech, the irregular heartwood formation is caused by vessel occlusion, oxidation, and dye deposits in the mature wood. The vessel occlusion results in poor impregnability. The most-common types are **red heartwood** and **pointed heartwood**. Red heartwood has a cloudy border, while pointed heartwood has a jagged or star like shape. Depending on the location, the onset of irregular heartwood can occur around an age of fifty to eighty years. Red heartwood and pointed heartwood are primarily color changes that do not significantly alter the physical properties.

Another type of abnormal heartwood formation is **brown heartwood**, common to ash trees. Here, the color change is caused by dye deposits in the storage cells.

Factors Due to External Influences

Cracks

In general, cracks occur when the body of wood is separated in the direction of the grain. On the cross-sectional surface, they run as radial cracks in the direction of the wood rays (medullary rays). In principle, there is a distinction among many different types of cracks—drying in particular leads to end cracks and surface cracks.

Shrinkage Cracks

Wood drying leads to a reduction of the water content in the wood below the fiber saturation point (approx. 30% wood moisture), which results in stresses and shrinkage cracks. These stresses often arise due to the different shrinkage dimensions in the longitudinal, radial, and tangential directions. The shrinkage dimensions differ more in heavy wood than in light wood, so the risk of shrinkage cracks forming is also greater. The risk of cracking depends largely on the felling time and the debarking condition.

Frost Cracks

Frost cracks occur in the outer parts of the trunk during sudden periods of frost, but they can sometimes penetrate to the pith. Hardwoods such as ash, oak, yew, elm, hornbeam, and maple are at risk, especially those with wide wood rays.

Dry Cracks and Heat Cracks

They occur on standing trees during long periods of drought. A drop in water content below the fiber saturation point leads to longitudinal cracks that can penetrate into the center of the wood.

Heartwood Cracks (Ray, Radial, Heart, and Pith Cracks)

Heartwood cracks run radially from the pith and expand considerably in the longitudinal direction of the trunk. Heartwood cracks are caused by external influences such as wind, snow pressure, slope inclination, one-sided crowns, etc.

Ring Shakes

This is caused by differences in tension in the wood caused by severe frost, heat, wind, or fungi. The annual rings partially separate from each other. Wood with severe ring shakes is unusable as sawn timber and can be used only for chemical processing (pulping) or as firewood.

Shrinkage crack.

Radial crack.

Ring shakes.

FACTORS DUE TO EXTERNAL INFLUENCES

Man-Made Damage

In addition to the three groups of wood characteristics described here, humans can also be a damaging factor. This includes damage deliberately done, some of which is unavoidable, mostly during forest management. The tree reacts to a wound by forming a barrier to prevent the penetration of air and thus a fungal infestation. A callus forms at the edge of the wound, which covers the wound and closes it completely.

The effectiveness of this wound healing is highly dependent on the tree species and the time of year when the damage occurs. The healing process is most effective in spring and late summer. If the wound is closed well and in good time, the wound area becomes discolored, disturbing the fiber structure. However, if this is not the case, extensive decay occurs, which the tree is no longer able to overcome. The thickness growth of the tree is restricted by the progressing rot.

Through the same overgrowth process, shrubs or closely spaced trees can also grow together, where one overgrows the other.

A callus is formed at the wound edge . . .

. . . which covers and closes the wound.

Closely spaced trees that have grown together.

Ingrown Foreign Objects

Foreign objects, such as fences and trees, can sometimes get into the wood. Over time, these become covered over and are no longer visible from the outside.

Ingrown fragments from projectile objects are the most common. However, foreign objects can also be of natural origin.

These foreign objects are usually visible only after the wood has been cut open or cut to size in the workshop. At the latest, however, they come to light while planing, which is of great annoyance to the craftsman. Ingrown foreign objects pose an accident risk to the people working with them, not to mention damage to the processing tools. In the wood itself, they cause changes to the fiber structure, discoloration, and rot.

A foreign ingrown branch.

Felling Damage

The felling of trees often results in damage to the undergrowth and neighboring trees. Grazing with a sharp or blunt object can also cause bark damage (or impact damage). These areas are often attacked by fungi (especially during summer felling), and rotting often occurs as a result. Further damage is caused by tears in the stressed, felled trunks or by tears due to incorrect felling notches.

An ingrown sign.

Ingrown foreign objects are a danger to people and tools during processing.

Bark damage (impact damage) is susceptible to fungal attack.

MAN-MADE DAMAGE

Incorrect Felling Times

Failure to observe the correct felling times (summer felling) can easily lead to fungal infestation—for example, blue-stain fungus in pinewood. Hardwoods, especially maple and birch, are prone to discoloration.

In the case of beech, incorrect felling times lead to stumpiness. There is also a greater risk of insect infestation. Since the sap is in the wood, more and larger cracks appear during drying, which encourages insect infestation.

Due to the risk of damage, more and more companies are now paying attention to felling time as a factor. Framing a material as "moon wood" (felled during certain lunar phases) can also be a compelling sales strategy.

This trunk was damaged by human negligence.

Fungal infestation on summer-felled wood.

Transport Damage

Damage caused by transportation can occur, both to the timber being transported and to the remaining stock. The most-common types are splintering and contamination by stones and other foreign objects. The remaining stock is usually damaged by motorized transport, which creates entry points on the tree for fungi and insects. In most cases, this damage occurs on the base trunk and therefore greatly reduces salability.

Environmental Factors

Air pollution is primarily responsible for increasing deforestation. Today, tons of harmful substances (sulfur dioxide and nitrogen oxides) are released into the air. The wind picks up the pollutants and blows them through the forests. The leaves now act like an oversized filter. Many trees cannot withstand the pollution and die as a result. This results in a loss of growth, and a reduction in the quantity available. Secondary changes, such as false heartwood in beech trees, oak and elm dieback, and the wet heartwood of fir that results in impaired impregnability, are also the result. "Moon rings" are also partly attributed to environmental pollution. For us woodworkers, it's important to reduce emissions where we can. This is the only way we can protect plants, animals, and people from even greater damage.

Wildlife Damage

Damage Due to Game Browsing

This is damage caused by deer, elk, and other animals in the form of browsing, debarking, or velvet rubs. Damage caused by summer debarking is particularly important, since this damage leads to prolonged overgrowth processes that are accompanied by fungal infestation and decay. Heavy browsing can slow natural regeneration.

Damage by Wood-Destroying Insects

Wood pests are animal pests (insects) that use wood as a breeding ground or as food. The wood can be partially or completely destroyed in the process. In the following section, I will discuss both wood-breeding and bark-breeding insects. The habitat of the larvae is defined in each case.

All wood-destroying insects go through four stages during their development; the length of each stage is influenced by humidity and temperature.

Egg → Larva → Pupa → Beetle

The actual wood destroyers are the larvae (woodworms). Depending on the insect species, they live in the wood for two to several years, mainly in the sapwood. On average, they create a borehole with a distance of one body length per day. Depending on the type of pest, they infest either the living tree, stored or constructed wood, softwood, or hardwood.

Some pests also attack both types of wood. The pests are classified as follows:

- **Trunk wood pests:** Infest standing trees (e.g., spruce moth, pine moth, bark beetle, poplar longhorn beetle)
- **Storage wood pests:** Infest stored wood (e.g., wood wasp, longhorn beetle)
- **Building pests:** Infest installed wood (e.g., house longhorn beetle, death-watch beetle, wood wasp)

Female longhorn beetle.

Longhorn beetle larva.

Longhorn in the borehole.

Certain types of insects infect only living trees and can leave behind boreholes that reduce the value of the wood. Larvae that live longer, such as the wood wasp, can enter the structure during processing and fly out later. However, dry, installed wood is no longer infested by these insects.

The beetles that are dangerous are the ones that live in dry wood. The larvae, which live for years, destroy the entire cross section of the wood. The beetles lay several hundred eggs, from which the larvae hatch after two to four weeks. In some beetle species, it takes up to fifteen years for the larvae to pupate and the beetle to hatch. During this time, the larvae's life consists of nothing but eating, eating, eating.

Common Furniture Beetle

This beetle (*Anobium punctuatum*) is one of the most harmful beetle species. The larva, which is ¼" (6 mm) long when fully grown, is cream colored and slightly hairy. This worm attacks deciduous and coniferous wood as well as old furniture. Structural timbers (half-timbering, roof beams, stairs, and the like) are particularly at risk, especially when the wood moisture content is high and the temperature is moderate. The numerous flight holes ($1/32$"–$1/16$", or 1–2 mm in diameter) of this nail beetle perforate the surface of the wood. The irregularly running boreholes are filled with bore dust and small balls of excrement.

Greater Horntail

Greater horntail.

Common furniture beetle.

Common furniture beetle emergence holes.

The female greater horntail punctures the wood with her ovipositor and lays her eggs together with fungal spores. The larvae then feed on the wood processed by the fungus.

Carpenter Ant

The largest native ant, the carpenter ant, builds labyrinth-like nests several meters high in the heartwood of standing trees, especially spruces. In fallen trees, these nests remain intact for years.

Carpenter ant.

Bark beetle.

Labyrinth-like nests of the carpenter ant.

Bark Beetle

Bark beetles are also notorious. The smaller bark beetle attacks mainly the upper third (the crown) of spruce trees. The larger of the two, also known as the spruce bark beetle, also attacks the trunk of the spruce.

The female, a few millimeters in size, eats a vertical channel under the bark with lateral niches in which she then lays her eggs.

The larvae feed on the sap-bearing layers of the tree. Since this is the tree's lifeline, the infestation usually leads to the death of the tree.

The larvae eat horizontal channels, which they then widen at the end to form a pupal cradle. Depending on the climate and temperature, the beetles develop three to four weeks after laying their eggs. The hatched beetles then gnaw a flight hole through the bark in order to fly out.

Channel with lateral niches ...

... for laying eggs.

WILDLIFE DAMAGE

Wood Diseases

Wood diseases are damage caused by plant-based wood destroyers or wood dwellers. They penetrate the cell walls and can thereby destroy the cell wall (rot). Fungi act as decay pathogens. The fungi consist mainly of cell threads, which form a cotton-like fungal network (mycelium).

This runs through the wood or is visible on the surface. Mycelium produces the fungus body, a flat structure that varies in shape and color depending on the type of fungus. Food is absorbed by breaking down the wood cells, which destroys the wood. In particular, the fungus targets proteins and sugars. The fungi require a temperature of 59°F–86°F (15°C–30°C) and a wood moisture content of over 20% to develop. Reproduction takes place through spores that are dispersed from the ripe fungal bodies and transferred to other wood by wind, water, or insects.

The type of rot varies depending on where the infestation is located:

- **Trunk rot**
  Pathological infestation on a standing tree
  Types: Brown rot, white rot, ring rot, pine tree rot, root rot

Fungal rot penetrates the cell walls and destroys the wood cells.

- **Storage rot**
  Pathological infestation of wood in storage
  Types: Graying, bluing, red streaks, mildew decay
- **House rot**
  Pathological infestation of installed wood
  Types: Dry rot, brown cellar rot, white pore fungus

Trunk rot (above) and a wooden structure destroyed by dry rot (below).

General guidelines for the prevention of wood diseases:

- proper timber drying
- correct wood storage
- preventive construction measures
- construction wood protection (professional processing)
- chemical wood protection (wood preservatives)

WOOD CHARACTERISTICS

Spalting, popular in turning, is a phenomenon caused by various fungi. For more, see project, page 82.

Protecting the wood from moisture above 20% is the best way to counteract the destruction of wood by fungi. Dry rot can also moisten dry wood itself via its root strands (mycelium) and is therefore the most dangerous wood destroyer. These often-unwelcome wood destroyers are not always unwelcome to the creative woodturner, because they can be used to achieve attractive effects and create many artistic objects.

Wood-Destroying Fungi
Brown Rot
Also known as heartwood rot or destruction rot. Its fungi break down mainly cellulose and leave behind red-brown lignin. The affected wood is usually reddish brown in color. Brown rot occurs most frequently in coniferous wood.
Damage pattern: Cube-shaped short fractures; cell structure is destroyed.
Most important brown rot pathogen: dry rot

White Rot
It is also known as corrosion rot. It is caused by fungi that break down mainly lignin. The whitish cellulose remains.
Damage pattern: Wood becomes fibrous or spongy. Strength and weight decrease, no longer usable as construction timber.

Most important white rot pathogen: turkey tail

Simultaneous Decomposition
Cellulose and lignin decompose simultaneously.
Damage pattern: Wood discolored white, then complete decay due to the occurrence of several different types of fungi

Wood-Discoloring Fungi
There are about 300 different species of fungi. The fungus species live mainly from wood constituents (protein, starch, sugar, etc.). The wood substance (cell wall) is damaged only slightly if at all.

Blue Fungus
Blue fungus is the most important discoloration. It occurs mainly in pine, mostly in sapwood. However, infestation is also possible in other types of wood.
Damage pattern: Mainly unsightly bluish discoloration of the sapwood on the surface, but also deep in the wood. The fungal bodies can damage paintwork and cause it to flake off. Also occur very often as unsightly blue-brown stains on boards in posts where they have been stacked.

Blue fungus.

WOOD DISEASES

Sourcing Green Wood

It is best to work with freshly felled wood. A discussion with your local forestry bureau often makes it possible to fell shrubs and other wooded plants, or even small trees. You should also ask farmers, who often prune trees in the orchard in the spring. The best materials for turning green wood are usually found in simple brushwood piles. Firewood from felling work is also well suited for this purpose. It is generally easier to obtain green wood than dry wood. Small branch pieces, which would break during drying, are also ideal for green woodturning.

The best material for green woodturning can often be found in simple woodpiles.

Projects

- Small Turned Tree
- Long-Stemmed Cup
- Flower Vase
- Lidded Vessel
- Ball
- Bark Bowl
- Bark Bowl Variation
- Natural Plum Wood Bowl
- Natural Applewood Bowl
- Plate

The previous chapters covered suitable woods for green woodturning, the storage and preservation of these woods, and essential wood characteristics. Now it's time to make ten very different but attractive objects from green wood. Starting with a small turned tree, we then move on to turning an intricate long-stemmed cup, which also makes use of a unique bending technique. We will also make a ball, several elegant bowls with bark edges, a lidded vessel made from spalted wood, and a plate.

Bowls and dishes can be turned from various types of wood.

Small Turned Tree

Trees accompany us throughout our lives. The gift of a tree is associated with the old tradition of planting a tree when an important life event such as a birth or wedding takes place. Why not give a decorative, hand-turned tree as a gift? This piece can embellish many a windowsill or serve as a tree decoration at Christmastime. Particularly suitable woods are ash, lime, maple, hazelnut, and birch.

The Process

Cut the fresh round timber to approximately 7$\frac{7}{8}$" (200 mm) and clamp it between the drive center and the live center in the lathe. The workpiece is first turned round using the large chisel or the bowl gouge. **(figs. 1–2)**

Since the workpiece needs to be clamped "on the fly" to enable processing on the end grain, attach the chuck at one of the two ends. **(figs. 3–4)**

Clamp the wood in the jaw chuck and check for concentricity. **(figs. 5–6)**

Using the bowl gouge, which is perfectly suited for green wood, form a cone.

SMALL TURNED TREE

Start removing chips from the left-hand side and guide the tool toward the right-hand edge, forming a cone. **(figs. 7-9)**

Remove material step by step, making sure to maintain a straight line. The resulting shavings confirm a good cutting edge and the correct cutting angle. **(figs. 10-11)**

Lightly round the front tip so that there is still enough material available in this end area. **(figs. 12-13)**

On the left side, use the small gouge to form a groove that will make up the tree trunk. Make sure that the bevel of the tool always serves as a guide. **(figs. 14-18)**

Fig. 1

Fig. 2

Fig. 3

Fig. 4

Fig. 5

Fig. 6

Fig. 7

Fig. 8

Fig. 9

Fig. 10

Fig. 11

Fig. 12

SMALL TURNED TREE

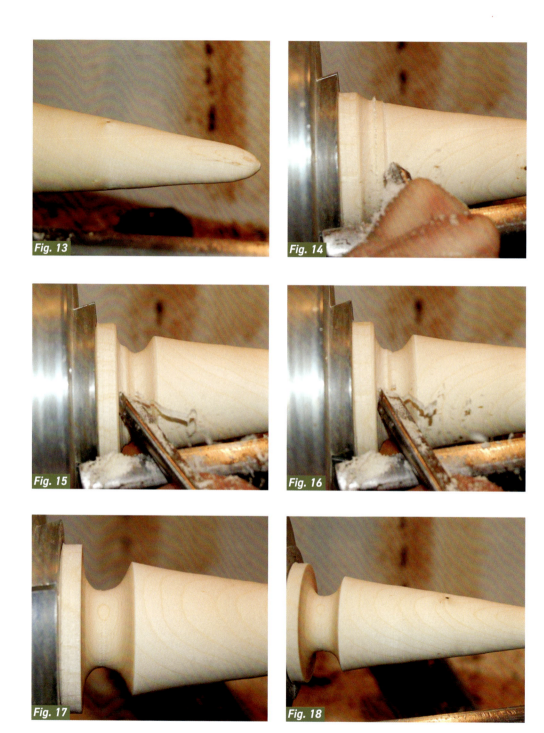

PROJECTS

Use the small or medium skew chisel to start turning the branch details. Hold the chisel at an angle to the axis of rotation and turn it slightly so that the bevel slides along the workpiece. As with finishing work, lift the tool until you remove a shaving. In contrast to finishing, shaving removal must remain concentrated in the area of the chisel. **(fig. 19)**

The chisel is now moved to the left-hand side, where you can continue to remove a series of small, even chips. You will immediately feel when the fiber can be lifted off with little effort. The length of the individual shavings depends on the moisture content of the wood, the type of wood, and the turner's patience. **(fig. 20)**

Lift the fibers one by one, turning each new sliver toward the previous one. Make sure the fibers are not too thick. **(figs. 21–24)**

As the diameter decreases, the shaving length also decreases. Process the front tip down to the smallest wood shaving. **(fig. 25)**

Fig. 19

Fig. 20

Fig. 21

Fig. 22

SMALL TURNED TREE

Fig. 23

Fig. 24

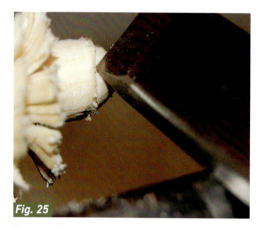
Fig. 25

Fig. 26

The tree is now turned and can be sawn off at the base with a handsaw. Remove any prominent cut marks with the edge sander. **(fig. 26)**

Long-Stemmed Cup

A special feature of turning green wood is that very thin objects can be made effortlessly, such as the stem of a cup. Every woodturner can determine the degree of difficulty themselves by making the handle thicker or thinner.

For this project, I used maple wood. It is particularly important to ensure that the heartwood of this raw piece is free of cracks and branches. In addition, the growth rings should run straight and smooth along the longitudinal axis. A prominent pith also makes it impossible to turn thin stems.

The Process

First, clamp a piece of wood approximately 12" (30 cm) long between the center punch and the face driver, turn it round, and create a tapered step on one side for clamping in the jaw chuck. **(fig. 1)**

Trim the entire length of the workpiece with the roughing gouge; alternatively, the large skew can also be used for smoothing. **(figs. 2–3)**

Now, turn the face or end grain flat with the medium gouge or the small chisel. The bevel of the tool rests on the workpiece so that it can be guided. **(fig. 4)**

Hollow the cup. The "overturning technique" is used for this. The overturning technique is used at the end grain for making goblets, egg cups, etc. If shavings are removed on the downward rotation when turning, when using the overturning technique, you will remove the shavings on the upward rotation. Use a small or medium gouge for this turning technique, keeping the sharpening angle rather blunt. Place the handrest at a right angle to the wood and slightly below the center. It is important that the inner shape is always turned before the outer shape; otherwise the oscillations and vibrations will be too strong and the end grain will no longer be malleable. With the gouge set at a light angle, turn a small depression in the center. **(fig. 5)**

Open the depression in the center by pressing the tool's cutting edge slightly forward and outward. Make sure to keep the cutting edge consistently in contact with the wood for a smooth opening. **(figs. 6–7)**

Repeat this technique until you have reached the desired depth. **(figs. 8–10)**

Fig. 1

Fig. 2

Fig. 3

Fig. 4

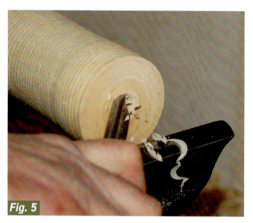

Fig. 5

Fig. 6

Fig. 7

Fig. 8

PROJECTS

Fig. 9

Fig. 10

Once the inner shape is finished and sanded, shape the outside of the project. First, determine the inside dimension and mark it on the outside with an allowance of ⅜" (1 cm). **(figs. 11–12)**

Turn a large, elongated channel to remove material. **(figs. 13–16)**

Form the outer contour with the small spindle gouge. The bevel of the tool slides along the workpiece and thus creates an almost wave-free surface. **(figs. 17–19)**

Create the stem (approximately ³⁄₁₆" or 4 mm in diameter) step by step. Make sure to remove only small chips at a time to avoid vibrations and possible breakage. **(fig. 20)**

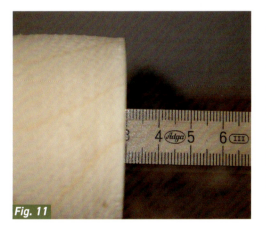
Fig. 11

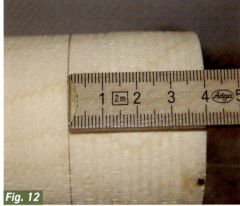
Fig. 12

LONG-STEMMED CUP

Fig. 13

Fig. 14

Fig. 15

Fig. 16

Fig. 17

Fig. 18

PROJECTS

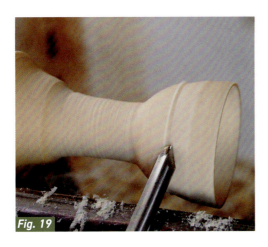
Fig. 19

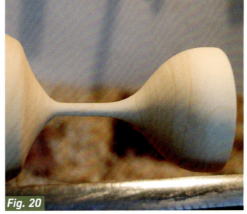
Fig. 20

The thinner the project, the more time you need to take for material removal. Impatience can lead to irreparable damage. A project's success can often depend on the woodturner's state of mind on a particular day. If you are in poor form, it is better not to practice woodturning, and to turn to other things instead.

Now you'll use a device called a steady rest, which enables the turning of thin, long stems. **(fig. 21)**

Such steady rests are available from specialty retailers in a wide variety of designs. I took the time to make one myself. It is a wooden bracket that is screwed together or, as here, connected with box joints. A board is attached to the underside, which fits within the bench bed. The bracket is mounted on the bench bed by using a wing nut, a screw, and a piece of plastic. The two jaws are attached to the upper part of the bracket, although these can also just be screwed on. The notches on the jaws, with a radius of $1/8$" (3 mm), were filed and will later hold the stem. **(fig. 22)**

I also built myself an extension, which makes it easy to create stems with a length of up to $15¾$" (400 mm) with a diameter of just $1/8$" (3 mm). The design of this device is variable—the only important thing is that the center of the notches sits exactly in the center of the axis of rotation. The best way to determine this dimension is to measure vertically from the lathe bed to the center point of the driver.

Mount the steady rest on the lathe bed and push the jaws toward the handle. **(figs. 23–24)**

Now turn the stem, first removing material with the gouge. **(figs. 25–27)**

Turn the finished diameter with the small chisel, holding the piece with the left hand to prevent the stem from vibrating. **(fig. 28)**

Rest the chisel on the project and remove the shavings from the middle of the cutting line. The fingers of the left hand clasp the workpiece, and the thumb rests on the tool. Slowly, in small steps and with little shaving removal, turn the handle and sand it down to the desired diameter. **(figs. 29–30)**

Fig. 21

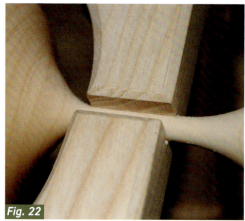
Fig. 22

Fig. 23

Fig. 24

Fig. 25

Fig. 26

PROJECTS

Fig. 27

Fig. 28

Fig. 29

Fig. 30

Fit the steady rest extension to facilitate the subsequent steps. **(figs. 31–32)** Remove material once again. **(fig. 33)**

A popular decoration for elongated woodwork is the "captured ring." This decoration surprises the observer and leaves them wondering how the ring was incorporated into the turner's work.

I will now turn such a ring by piercing the left and right with a small skew chisel. The size of the ring is determined by the diameter of the workpiece. **(figs. 34–36)**

Shape the round piece with the small detail gouge, taking care to ensure symmetry. **(figs. 37–38)**

Work the inside of the ring with the hook knife (I have reshaped mine from a small chisel). **(fig. 39)**

Next, pierce the piece from the left and right alternately, working in a circle. Once the ring has separated from the rest of the wood, it can be pushed forward. **(figs. 40–42)**

LONG-STEMMED CUP

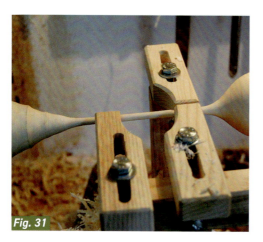
Fig. 31

Fig. 32

Fig. 33

Fig. 34

Fig. 35

Fig. 36

PROJECTS

Fig. 37

Fig. 38

Fig. 39

Fig. 40

Fig. 41

Fig. 42

Attach this to the steady rest, using adhesive tape so that it does not interfere during further processing. **(fig. 43)** Now turn the stem a little more, using the gouge and the chisel. **(figs. 44–46)**

Set the steady rest extensions slightly forward. **(figs. 47–48)**

Use the gouge to form a groove at the end of the stem, which forms the transition to the base. **(figs. 49–50)**

Use the small skew chisel to determine the height of the pedestal, piercing it with the tip of the chisel. **(fig. 51)**

Turn and sand the long-stemmed cup. **(figs. 52–53)**

Separate the workpiece from the rest of the wood by using a fine saw, such as a Japanese pull saw. **(figs. 54–56)**

Sand the end-grain surface of the base on the belt sander, paying attention to possible heat development to avoid dry cracks. **(figs. 57–58)**

The turned ring can either lie on the base or be glued to the stem. **(figs. 59–60)**

Bending the stem is another creative shaping technique. **(fig. 61)**

Fig. 43

Fig. 44

Fig. 45

Fig. 46

Fig. 47

Fig. 48

Fig. 49

Fig. 50

Fig. 51

Fig. 52

LONG-STEMMED CUP

Fig. 53

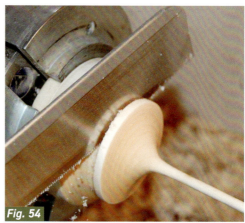

Fig. 54

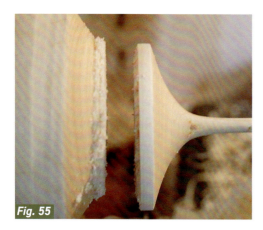

Fig. 55

Fig. 56

Fig. 57

Fig. 58

Fig. 59

Fig. 60

Fig. 61

Michael Thonet was already working on bending wood in 1830. Some of his unique bentwood furniture can still be found in many a coffee shop today. Suitable woods for this are beech, ash, oak, basswood or lime, and birch. When bending wood, the inner side is compressed, and the outer side is stretched. In contrast to stretching, compression is not a problem. Wood has the characteristic of being easily compressed. Lengthening wood is much more difficult, however, since the risk of breakage is very high. When you're bending wood, the organic substance called lignin, which is stored in the cell wall, plays an important role. Lignin serves as a strengthening element of the cell and is responsible for its lignification. If the lignin is softened, the wood cells can be moved against each other when bent. After drying, these cells interlock again, and the shape remains stable. The conditions for reshaping are best when the wood is wet. A pipe, which has been sealed at one end, is filled with boiling water. This pipe now serves as a bending iron of sorts. The workpiece turned from fresh wood can now be shaped around the pipe by hand.

Make sure the contact pressure remains even. Bend the stem gradually, using a lot of patience. **(figs. 62–66)**

Fig. 62

LONG-STEMMED CUP

Fig. 63

Fig. 64

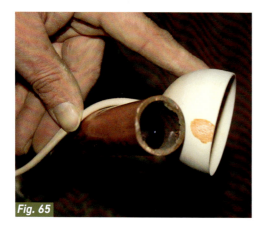
Fig. 65

Fig. 66

The heat from the pipe dries the inside faster than the outside, which eases the bending process. The shape typically becomes stable after just a few minutes.

Always be aware of the burning risk from the hot pipe.

It is particularly important that the wood being bent is wet enough. Sometimes wood that has been felled in the winter or stored for too long can no longer be bent. This can be fixed by steaming. However, make sure that the wood has a residual moisture content of at least 20%–30%. **(fig. 67)**

Steam the workpiece in a large cook pot for one hour. This softens the lignin and enables bending. **(fig. 68)**

Bend the workpiece around the pipe. **(figs. 69–70)**

The wood cells must be given time to shift. Bending too quickly will inevitably lead to fiber breakage. It is also important to create counter-pressure with your fingers on the outside. Bending should be done with moderate, even pressure.

Take special care when crossing the two ends. **(figs. 71–73)**

PROJECTS

Once the workpiece has reached the desired shape, secure it in place by using binding wire. **(fig. 74)**

After one to two days, the wire can be removed, and the workpiece can be removed from the bending mold. **(fig. 75)**

When bending a whole circle, make sure that the ratio between the diameter of the stem and the diameter of the pipe is approximately 1:10. This means that if the diameter of the stem is $^3/_{16}$" (4 mm), the pipe diameter should be approx. $1^9/_{16}$" (40 mm).

However, this is only a rule of thumb; the flexibility of a piece of wood is heavily dependent on the moisture content, structure, and quality of that wood.

Also note that the cup stem must be at least 3.14 times as long as the pipe diameter. **(fig. 76)**

With a lot of patience, a few tries, and a few setbacks, you will gain the necessary experience to bend wood easily and thus create valuable heirlooms-to-be.

Fig. 67

Fig. 68

Fig. 69

LONG-STEMMED CUP

Fig. 70

Fig. 71

Fig. 72

Fig. 73

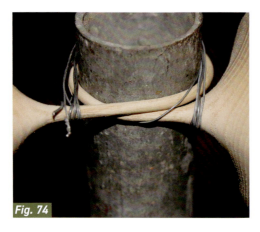
Fig. 74

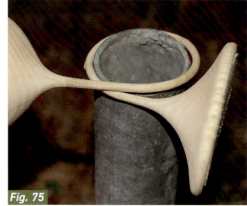
Fig. 75

Fig. 76

Flower Vase

Vases are another project beloved by woodturners. These can vary so widely in shape, size, and execution that there are almost no limits to what you can do. I have chosen cherry wood for this piece.

The Process

Clamp the wood in the jaw chuck, straighten it, and turn it flat on the end-grain surface. **(figs. 1–2)** Since the inside of the vase will be carved out, make a notch with the tip of the skew chisel in the center of the turning axis on the end grain. This is to guide the drill and give it the necessary hold. **(figs. 3–4)** Insert a drill chuck in the tail spindle of the tailstock. Extract the material with a drill bit. **(figs. 6–7)**

With the small gouge, pull the upper edge slightly outward, then remove the chips on the left side of the cutting line. **(figs. 8–9)**. Turn off the lathe and determine the length of the workpiece by adding $3/8$" (1 cm) to the inside dimension and marking that new dimension on the outside with a pencil. **(figs. 10–11)** Then, turn the lathe back on and make a notch along that dimension line with a small chisel. **(fig. 12)**

Fig. 1

Fig. 2

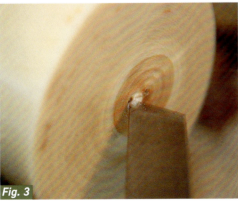
Fig. 3

Fig. 4

Fig. 5

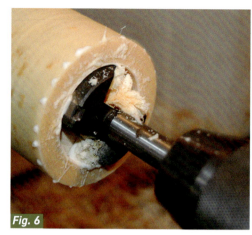
Fig. 6

Fig. 7

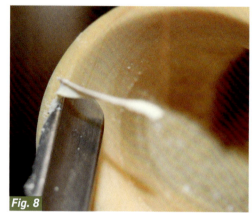
Fig. 8

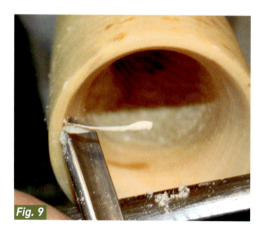
Fig. 9

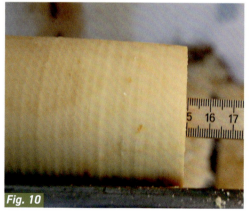
Fig. 10

Fig. 11

Fig. 12

Now turn the vase to a wall thickness of 1/16" (2 mm). The small, medium, or large gouge can be used for this. Always pay attention to the correct turning technique; this avoids unsightly tears and vibrations. **(figs. 13–14)**

To check the finished wall thickness and uniformity, first feel it with your fingers, placing your thumb in the hole and the remaining fingers on the outside of the vase. Then make the individual corrections step by step with a small gouge. **(figs. 15–16)**

One of the most important aids when turning green wood is light. Light sources can be used to make the individual material thicknesses visible. I made a lamp insert for the tailstock for this purpose. This consists of a cone that sits in the tail spindle. A standard lightbulb socket is attached via a drilled hole. Another hole is used to route the power cord. **(fig. 17)**

The lamp can now be cranked continuously into the vase, using the handwheel. **(fig. 18)**

You can clearly see the material thickness with the light, since thick walls appear darker than thin ones. Turn the small gouge evenly and gradually until the material appears equally light all around. **(figs. 19–21)**

A good cutting edge and even, gradual shaving removal guarantee successful results. **(figs. 22–23)**

Sand the workpiece with a sanding screen, which is ideal for green wood. **(fig. 24)**

Fig. 13

Fig. 14

FLOWER VASE

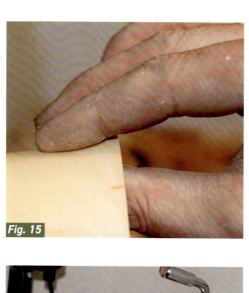
Fig. 15

Fig. 16

Fig. 17

Fig. 18

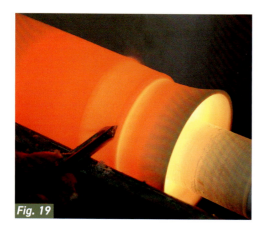
Fig. 19

Fig. 20

PROJECTS

Fig. 21

Fig. 22

Fig. 23

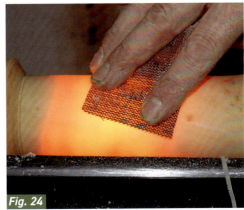
Fig. 24

Stuck sanding material caused by the wood moisture can be cleaned from behind using compressed air. **(figs. 25–27)**

This sanding residue can also be washed out in a bucketful of water. The base of the vase can be easily recognized through the translucent light and can be made even thinner if necessary. Use the small skew chisel to make a notch approx. ³⁄₈" (10 mm) wide. **(figs. 28–30)** A small rounding at the edge of the base, achieved with the small detail gouge, ensures a harmonious finish. **(fig. 31)**

Sand the rounded edge and cut the vase with a fine saw. Sand the base flat with the edge sander. **(figs. 32–34)**

FLOWER VASE

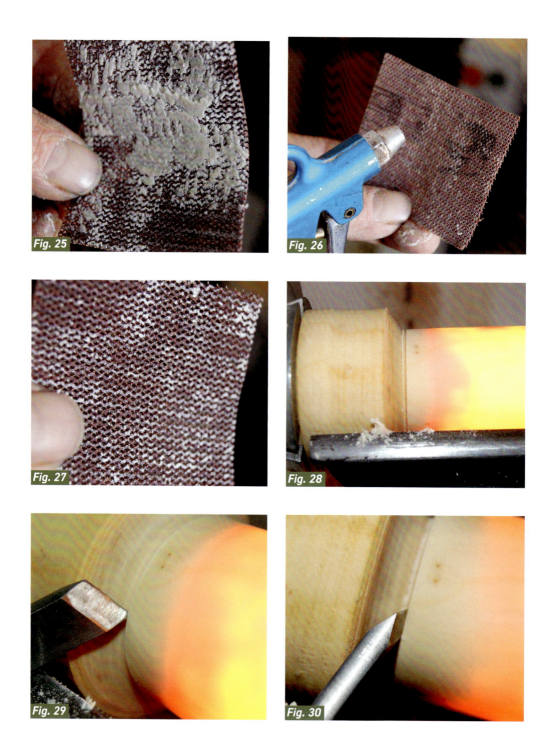

PROJECTS

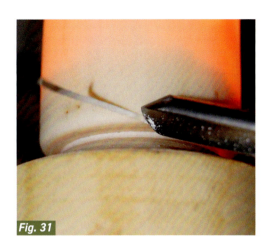
Fig. 31

Fig. 32

Fig. 33

Fig. 34

FLOWER VASE

Lidded Vessel

This project doesn't have to be made from green wood, but due to the many interesting steps, as well as clamping technique and working methods, I do not want to neglect this topic. Fungal infestation or insect infestation, in some cases even both, give this workpiece a special touch. These types of woods are very popular with woodturners due to their special markings. Beech or birch is best suited for the features I'll describe.

Storing wood for multiple months on wet ground...

... forms mildew on the wood.

Fungus-infested wood, also known as spalted wood, is easy to produce. Since the necessary fungal spores are already present in the wood, they need only to be further developed. These fungi produce fruiting bodies on the outside. The strongly pronounced edges and color differences are a defensive reaction between the individual fungi. Since they require moisture, the piece of wood can simply be stored for several months in damp ground without exposure to sunlight.

A second, quicker option is to pack the damp wood in a plastic bag. Let time pass and check weekly until the wood has acquired the desired look.

During processing, take care to ensure that you do not inhale any sawdust, since this can harm your respiratory health. It is therefore essential to wear a commercially available dust mask whenever you'll be producing sawdust.

Cut the wood to size on the bandsaw. It is important to check whether unwanted drying cracks have formed at the edges of the end grain. Depending on the type of drying, these may be more or less pronounced.

Cutting the wood to size with a saw.

PROJECTS

The Process

Clamp the workpiece between the drive center and the live center and turn it almost round. There should still be a small, flat area left so that the workpiece can rest securely on the bandsaw later, minimizing risk of injury. The grain of the wood should run from the lid to the base. **(figs. 1–2)**

Turn a conical base on the left and right sides of the workpiece; you'll use this for clamping in the jaw chuck later. **(figs. 3–4)**

Use the bandsaw to separate the lid from the container, with the flat area resting on the machine table to prevent the wood from turning. **(fig. 5)**

First, clamp the lid in the chuck. **(fig. 6)**

Use the small detail gouge to turn the front wood surface flat. Pierce the cutting line with the tip, turn the tube slightly open, and turn toward the center. The bevel slides along the workpiece to achieve maximum control. **(figs. 7–8)**

Bring the workpiece to the desired diameter. **(figs. 9–10)**

Hollow out the lid on the inside and reduce the speed to minimize heat on the workpiece. **(fig. 11)**

Using the tip of the large chisel, turn the inside of the piece to completion. **(figs. 12–14)** Measure the length with a ruler and mark it with a pencil. **(figs. 15–16)**

Make a notch with the small skew chisel to set the length. **(fig. 17)**

Insert the small skew chisel, and form the round shape with the small gouge. **(figs. 18–19)**

The outer shape of the lid is now complete. Create a rounded lip along the top of the lid. **(figs. 20–22)**

Fig. 1

Fig. 2

Fig. 3

Fig. 4

PROJECTS

Fig. 5

Fig. 6

Fig. 7

Fig. 8

Fig. 9

Fig. 10

LIDDED VESSEL

Fig. 11

Fig. 12

Fig. 13

Fig. 14

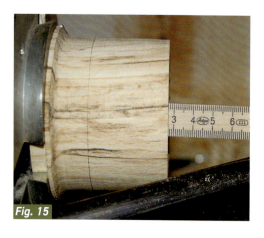
Fig. 15

Fig. 16

PROJECTS

Fig. 17

Fig. 18

Fig. 19

Fig. 20

Fig. 21

Fig. 22

LIDDED VESSEL

Saw the workpiece off with a fine saw, such as a Japanese pull saw. **(figs. 23–25)**

Next, clamp the piece of wood for the vessel and smooth it with the skew chisel. Remove the shavings in the lower third of the cutting line and slide the bevel along the workpiece to achieve a perfect surface. **(figs. 26–27)**

Measure the inside dimension of the lid with a vernier caliper to determine the tenon size of the vessel. **(fig. 28)**

This tenon then serves as a clamping device for processing the lid. Create the tenon with the small chisel. Use the tip of this chisel to make an angled notch.

Remove the shavings along the grain with the chisel. **(figs. 29–31)**

Use the vernier caliper to measure and make adjustments if necessary, ensuring that the cover fits snugly, so that it provides a firm hold during future steps.

A small groove on the edge of the tenon makes it easier to fit the lid. **(figs. 32–34)**

Fig. 23

Fig. 24

Fig. 25

Fig. 26

PROJECTS

Fig. 27

Fig. 28

Fig. 29

Fig. 30

Fig. 31

Fig. 32

LIDDED VESSEL

Fig. 33

Fig. 34

Now the front of the lid can be shaped effortlessly. Do this with the small gouge, moving from the edge toward the center. **(figs. 35-37)**

Sand the workpiece, using 120- and then 150-grit sandpaper or emery cloth. **(figs. 38-39)**

Hollow the vessel and then measure and mark the length. **(figs. 40-41)**

Turn the edge with the large chisel to achieve the correct dimensions and a clean surface. **(figs. 42-43)**

Use the small chisel to generously pierce the bottom of the vessel. **(fig. 44)**

Measure the diameter of the lid so that it can be adjusted to the vessel. **(figs. 45-48)**

The outer shape can now be finished with the small gouge. Make sure to remove only a small amount of shavings, to prevent the workpiece from vibrating, which could result in breakage or an unsightly surface. **(figs. 49-50)** The vessel is then sanded. **(fig. 51)**

Fig. 35

Fig. 36

PROJECTS

Fig. 37

Fig. 38

Fig. 39

Fig. 40

Fig. 41

Fig. 42

LIDDED VESSEL

Fig. 43

Fig. 44

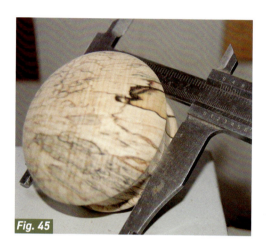
Fig. 45

Fig. 46

Fig. 47

Fig. 48

PROJECTS

Fig. 49

Fig. 50

Fig. 51

To make a simple sanding aid, cut into the end of a round wood dowel with a saw and insert a bit of sandpaper or emery cloth. The diameter of the round rod must be significantly smaller than the opening you'll be sanding. Since the sandpaper is not attached any other way, the paper can be easily replaced as needed. With this aid, sand the inside of the vessel. **(figs. 52–53)**

Separate the workpiece from the remaining wood using the fine saw, and sand the bottom flat on the belt sander. **(figs. 54–57)**

The vessel and the lid are made from one piece of wood, with the markings running through from the lid to the base. **(fig. 58)**

Fig. 52

LIDDED VESSEL

PROJECTS

Ball

Balls are not only popular toys, but also decorative pieces of art. This ball was made from cherry wood. Knots, growths, and other wood features are welcome in this project, since they add to its beauty.

The Process

Clamp the wet piece of wood in the lathe and turn it round. Since the piece is not round, pay particular attention to the correct speed and the correct setting for the handrest. **(fig. 1)**

Slowly guide the bowl gouge along the workpiece until the shavings are removed. After a few passes, the wood is turned round and can be brought to the correct diameter. **(figs. 2–3)**

Measure the diameter of the turned barrel with the vernier caliper and mark it lengthwise. **(figs. 4–5)**

Use the small skew chisel to cut left and right, alternating between straight and angled cuts with the tip of the tool. **(figs. 6–8)**

Using a pencil, mark the middle of the ball. **(fig. 9)**

Two templates are made from a $3/16$" (4 mm) thick sheet of plywood by using a jigsaw, one for the outer shape and the other for the chuck of the ball. **(fig. 10)**

The ball is shaped with the middle gouge. The bevel of the tool rests on the wood to achieve a clean surface. **(fig. 11)**

Once one half is finished, turn the second half. **(figs. 12–13)**

Use the template to check the turned contour. **(fig. 14)**

Fig. 1

Fig. 2

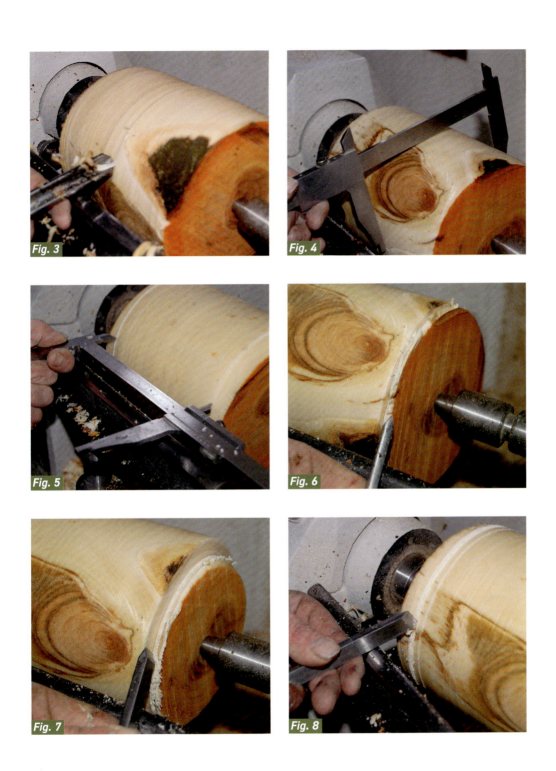

97

BALL

Fig. 9

Fig. 10

Fig. 11

Fig. 12

Fig. 13

Fig. 14

PROJECTS

Use the pencil to mark the areas that still have too much material. **(fig. 15)**

Gradually correct the shape step by step, referring regularly to the template. **(figs. 16–17)**

Small grooves and irregularities can be carefully scraped away at the end, using the large skew chisel. Since this work step involves scraping off shavings, ensure that your cutting edge is sharp and free of blemishes. **(fig. 18)**

If the ball matches the semicircle of the template, turn a small depression in the form of a groove in the middle. This should be only about 1/16"–1/8" (2–3 mm) deep. **(figs. 19–22)**

Now unclamp the ball and saw the ends off. **(fig. 23)**

Dry wood must be used for the chuck of the ball. I chose birchwood because it is less likely to crack dramatically, even in large dimensions. Clamp the wood again with the jaw chuck and turn it flat. **(fig. 24)**

Fig. 15

Fig. 16

Fig. 17

Fig. 18

BALL

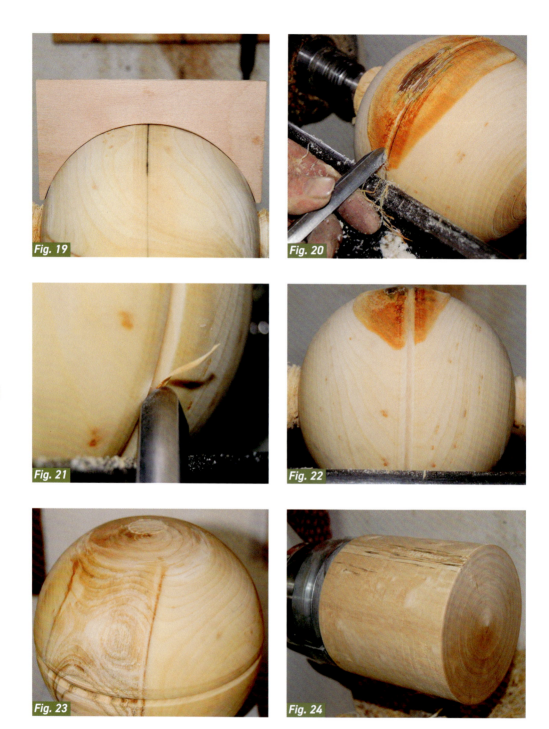

Fig. 19

Fig. 20

Fig. 21

Fig. 22

Fig. 23

Fig. 24

PROJECTS

Hollow out the negative shape of the sphere, using the overturning technique. **(figs. 25–26)**

Use the pointed compass to measure the sphere. The left-hand point of the compass is used to make a mark, and the right-hand point is used as the control. **(fig. 27)**

Since the ball should not sit in the chuck up to the middle, the chuck diameter should measure 3/16" (5 mm) less than the diameter of the ball. If the ball is clamped up to the middle, a smooth curve is not possible. Turn the clamping device, using a great deal of patience and constant checking against the template. **(figs. 28–30)**

Turn the ball 90 degrees and clamp it in the finished chuck. This turning technique guarantees a perfectly round ball. Make a light tap with the hammer, and the ball is in place. **(figs. 31–32)**

Anyone who thinks this won't hold is mistaken. The more precisely the two contours match, the tighter the ball sits in the chuck. It often takes many blows on the chuck with a hammer to loosen the ball again.

Position the ball precisely, using the tailstock and the center point of the live center. The turned groove must run exactly along the axis of rotation. The center point of the center punch must meet the groove. **(fig. 33)**

Fig. 25

Fig. 26

Fig. 27

Fig. 28

BALL

Fig. 29

Fig. 30

Fig. 31

Fig. 32

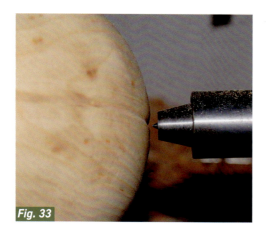
Fig. 33

Fig. 34

PROJECTS

Use the small gouge to start turning from the center. Slowly and in small steps, remove material up to the groove. If you turn deeper than the groove, the ball can no longer be exactly round. The groove therefore represents the depth limit. **(figs. 34–36)**

Frequent checking and perfect chip removal are guarantees for success. **(figs. 37–38)**

As mentioned previously, try to work slightly above the middle to create a nice transition between the two halves. **(fig. 39)**

It is wise to leave a trace of the groove, which can then be sanded away with sandpaper. This makes it possible to work symmetrically and prevents the removal of too much material. Finally, use the large skew chisel to finely scrape away any unsightly ridges. **(figs. 40–41)**

Fig. 35

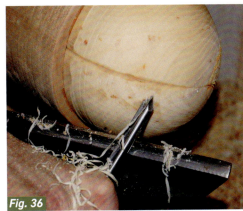
Fig. 36

Fig. 37

Fig. 38

Fig. 39

Fig. 40

Fig. 41

Fig. 42

Fig. 43

Fig. 44

PROJECTS

Fig. 45

Fig. 46

Fig. 47

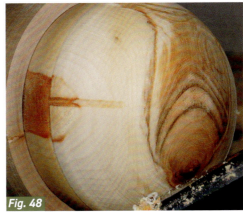
Fig. 48

Unclamp the ball; you've now finished one half. **(fig. 42)**

With the small gouge, turn the chuck again and adjust to the smaller diameter. Patience and precision guarantee that the ball is held securely. **(figs. 43–44)**

Check the fit of the ball several times before securing it. Then clamp it to finish turning the second half. **(fig. 45)**

Now carry out the same steps as for the first half of the ball. Always ensure that the shavings are removed evenly for a clean, ridge-free surface. Better to get the contour right while turning than to try fixing large mistakes with sandpaper later. **(figs. 46–48)**

BALL

Fig. 49

Fig. 50

Fig. 51

Fig. 52

Fig. 53

Once the ball is done being turned, sand it by using a sanding screen. **(fig. 49)**

Clamp the ball crosswise and resand it. **(figs. 50–52)**

If a ball is to remain dimensionally stable and free from deformation, it must be made of dry wood. Balls made of green wood are merely ornamental objects, which, made of different types of wood and in different sizes, decorate many a vestibule, entrance, or living room. **(fig. 53)**

Bark Bowl

Bowls with natural wood rims are popular, decorative, and functional workpieces for green woodturning. Live-edge bowls exude a special charm. The bark remaining on the workpiece connects the piece to its origin—the tree.

The Process

I made this project from birchwood. First, cut the wood lengthwise with a bandsaw. **(fig. 1)**

The diameter of the piece of wood is also the length of the project. **(figs 2–3)**

Saw the block to a round shape. Since the round side of the raw piece cannot be marked precisely with a pencil compass, a tool is used here to assist. Cut a circle with the desired diameter out of thick cardboard or plywood board. **(figs. 4–5)**

Hammer a nail into the exact center of this circle and fasten it to the wood. **(fig. 6)** It is now safe to cut in a circle along the template. **(fig. 7)**

Drill a hole with the drill press, using the nail hole to guide the center point of the drill. **(fig. 8)**

The jaws of the chuck can be swapped out for different sizes or types. Attach these jaws to the chuck with screws. **(fig. 9)**

Position the project and clamp it by widening the jaws. The ribbed clamping jaws provide additional support. **(fig. 10)**

Fig. 1

Fig. 2

Fig. 3

Fig. 4

Fig. 5

Fig. 6

PROJECTS

Fig. 7

Fig. 8

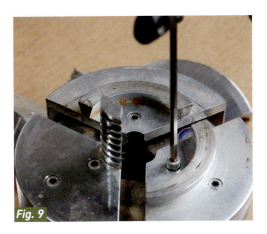
Fig. 9

Fig. 10

Once the correct speed has been set and the handrest has been mounted correctly, you can start turning. The first step is to turn the workpiece round, using the bowl gouge. Since the wood is still very unstable at the beginning, remove the shavings patiently, in small steps. **(figs. 11-12)**

Turn the front face flat. Start working from the center, since this is the smoothest running point of the surface. Then lead the tool to the outer edge. **(figs. 13-14)**

Mark the diameter of the base, using dividers. **(fig. 15)**

Remove material in order to prepare the support for the base. **(fig. 16)**

Use the small gouge to form the slightly conical base. **(fig. 17)**

The bowl gouge is used to shape the outer contour of the bowl. Since green wood can be sanded only to a limited extent, only a clean and almost ridge-free turned surface guarantees a perfect workpiece.

BARK BOWL

It is therefore important that the bevel glides continuously across the wood to guarantee a continuous cut. Once the necessary material has been removed, the outer shape of the bowl should be turned in a single pass. **(figs. 18-19)**

Once the project has been sanded, reclamp it and then change the jaws of the chuck. **(figs. 20-21)**

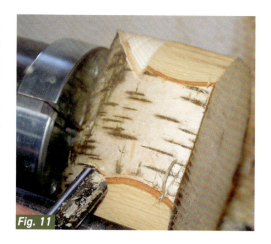
Fig. 11

Fig. 12

Fig. 13

Fig. 14

Fig. 15

PROJECTS

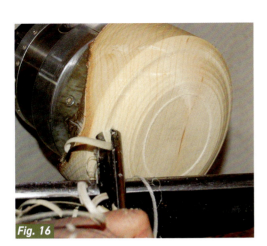
Fig. 16

Fig. 17

Fig. 18

Fig. 19

Fig. 20

Fig. 21

BARK BOWL

In the next steps, you will hollow the inside of the bowl with the bowl gouge. Remove the material in small steps, starting from the inside. Hold the gouge at a slight angle, turned slightly upward, and guide it to the center in an arching motion. **(figs. 22–26)**

Carefully turn the edge to an approximate thickness of $^{3}/_{16}$" (5 mm) with the small gouge. Remove shavings carefully to prevent possible vibration, which can lead to workpiece breakage or unsightly ridges. Special care is required, since the shape of the bark means that the cutting edge alternates from the air back to the material during turning. **(fig. 27)**

When making the bottom of the bowl, make sure that there is a smooth transition. You should therefore start by rounding between the edge and the base as soon as possible, since this can be re-turned at any time. **(figs. 28–30)**

Repeatedly feel the wall thickness with your fingers and correct it if necessary. Now that the bowl is sanded, reduce the speed so that the uneven edge can also be sanded.

Fig. 22

Fig. 23

Fig. 24

Fig. 25

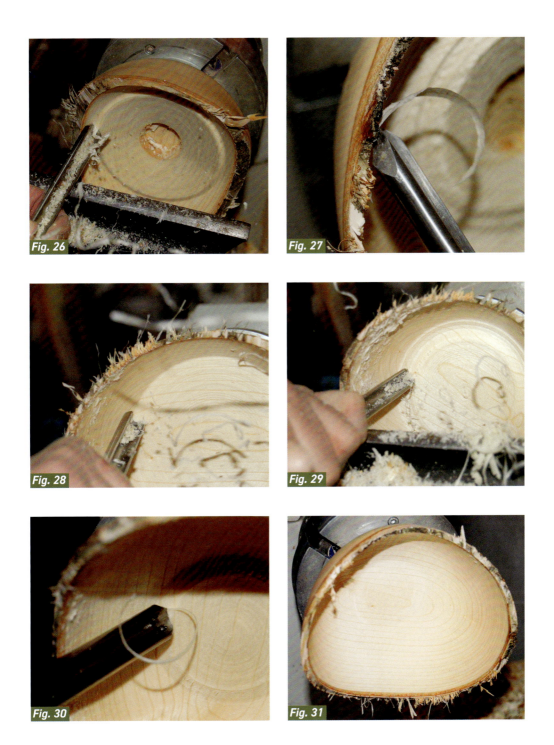

BARK BOWL

If deeper marks and impurities are visible, these can also be addressed when the machine is stopped. **(figs. 31–33)**

The easiest way, however, is to sand when the piece is dry. Drying such bowls takes only a few days. Due to the low material thickness, there is no risk of cracking. The shell will become distorted only due to the different shrinkage dimensions in the longitudinal and transverse wood. If you measure a bark bowl when it is dry, you will notice that it has become more ovular. Since the base and therefore the standing surface of the bowl also warps during drying, it must be smoothed on the belt sander.

Fig. 32

Fig. 33

PROJECTS

Bark Bowl Variation

Let's turn to a variation on a natural-edge bowl. While the diameter and length of the previous workpiece are identical, the ratio is different in the following bowl. The length is much greater than the diameter. For this reason, certain rules must be observed during machining to avoid accidents. The thickness of the wood to be worked is also only about $3/16$" (4–5 cm).

The Process

Use the pencil compass to draw the curves at both ends. The radius of the curves is half the total length of the workpiece. As you did in the prior project, drill a hole for clamping. **(figs. 1–2)**

Trim the wood with the bandsaw and clamp it onto the pin jaws of the jaw chuck. In contrast to circular bowls, instead of turning the workpiece round first, you'll form the outer contour immediately by removing material with the bowl gouge. The noncircular outer contour creates a certain imbalance, which can be compensated for by reducing the speed. The "danger area" between the handrest and the unsteady workpiece should always be treated with respect.

Fig. 1

Fig. 2

Fig. 3

Fig. 4

Fig. 5

Fig. 6

PROJECTS

With a good cutting edge, it is an experience to be able to shape green wood like butter. If you see long shavings, this is a sign that you're following the technique correctly. **(figs. 3-5)** Then, prepare a flat surface for the base. **(fig. 6)**

Mark the base dimension and turn the base. **(figs. 7-9)**

The ridge-free design of the outer shape is made possible by the correct turning technique, in which the bevel of the tool rests on the wood and the shaving lifts easily. **(figs. 10-13)**

Make sure to prepare for the changing shaving removal due to the irregular shape of the workpiece. Sand the shell and remove protruding bark pieces with a knife. **(figs. 14-16)**

Remove the bowl from the mandrel and clamp it with the jaw chuck. **(fig. 17)**

Again, start turning the bowl from the center. **(figs. 18-20)**

The following photos show how the cutting edge is alternately in the air and then plunges back into the wood. **(figs. 21-23)**

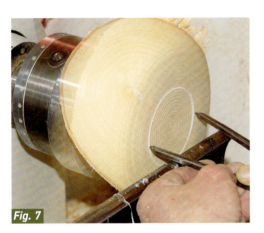
Fig. 7

Fig. 8

Fig. 9

Fig. 10

BARK BOWL VARIATION

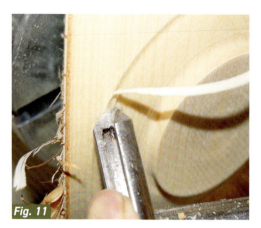
Fig. 11

Fig. 12

Fig. 13

Fig. 14

Fig. 15

Fig. 16

PROJECTS

BARK BOWL VARIATION

One particular danger zone is the area between the workpiece and the handrest. Do not underestimate the risks associated with this area! If you get your fingers in this zone, serious injuries can occur.

Set the bowl rim with the small gouge and then turn it with the bowl gouge in one pass to the center. **(figs. 24–28)**

When sanding, make sure that you do not work past the transition from the edge to the base; otherwise, injuries could occur. The rough and irregular edge is hard on the fingers. The edge is best sanded by hand after the bowl has dried. **(figs. 29–31)**

This slightly flatter bark bowl can be used to decorate pieces of furniture. This bowl can also be used as a functional piece, to hold keys and other small items.

Fig. 23

Fig. 24

Fig. 25

Fig. 26

PROJECTS

Fig. 27

Fig. 28

Fig. 29

Fig. 30

Fig. 31

BARK BOWL VARIATION

Natural Plum Wood Bowl

As already mentioned, you can find useful material in many piles of scrap wood—such as this plum wood, which is highly decorative due to its intense coloring.

The Process

To protect the cutting edge of my tool, I brush the bark with a wire brush. This removes any dirt. **(fig. 1)**

A faceplate is then screwed onto the piece of wood, which is then mounted on the lathe spindle. The faceplate must be screwed on completely so that it sits firmly against the spindle. **(fig. 2)**

Because of the irregular outer contour of the shell, take special care while turning. **(fig. 3)**

The handrest must be adjusted so that it sits as close as possible to the workpiece but never touches it. Therefore, before you start the machine, do a test run by hand. Adjust the position of the handrest on the basis of the size of the workpiece. **(figs. 4–5)**

The greatest danger zone is the area between the handrest and the workpiece. Make sure to observe a proper turning speed to avoid injuries.

The first step is to turn the outside of the bowl. Use the bowl gouge to create the desired shape. Since this piece of wood is longitudinal, the shavings are removed from top to bottom. **(figs. 6–7)**

When cutting the outer edge, take special care. This delicate step is best carried out with a small gouge. Turn the gouge slightly outward and remove the shavings in the middle area of the cutting line. Using patience and concentration, remove a very small amount of wood, holding the tool firmly with both hands at all times. **(fig. 8)**

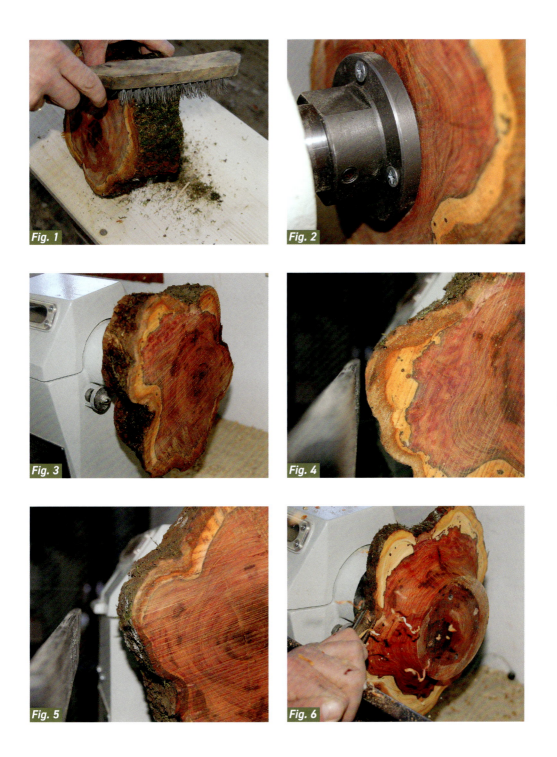

NATURAL PLUM WOOD BOWL

Fig. 7

Fig. 8

Turn the base flat from the outside in using the bowl gouge. Make sure that the bevel of the tool slides along the workpiece so that it can be easily maneuvered. **(figs. 9–10)**

Use the small gouge to turn the recess in the base, which is then used for clamping in the jaw chuck. Remove the shavings from the center outward. **(figs. 11–12)**

Reclamp the workpiece and then create the inner shape. **(fig. 13)**

First, turn the end grain flat with the bowl gouge. This step involves working from the outside toward the center. **(figs. 14–16)**

With the bowl gouge pointing slightly outward, turn out the inner shape, starting from the center. Patiently and gradually remove the material from the outside in, gradually guiding the tool in an arch toward the center. **(figs. 17–19)**

Repeat this step until you've achieved the desired edge thickness, and the inner contour matches the outer contour.

Fig. 9

Fig. 10

PROJECTS

Fig. 11

Fig. 12

Fig. 13

Fig. 14

Fig. 15

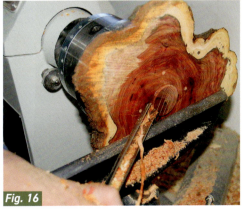
Fig. 16

NATURAL PLUM WOOD BOWL

Fig. 17

Fig. 18

Fig. 19

Fig. 20

It is important to use the correct turning technique and the correct shaving removal to achieve a clean surface. For this reason, I deliberately refrained from using abrasives on this workpiece. **(fig. 20)**

Since a great deal of stress is released with dense wood, take extra care during drying to avoid severe cracking. To do this, I wrap the workpiece in several layers of linen cloth, scattering dry wood shavings between layers. **(figs. 21–22)**

Now, hang the bag containing the wet workpiece in a dry place. **(fig. 23)**

After one to two weeks, unpack the workpiece and remove the shavings. **(figs. 24–26)**

Since the wood is now dry, the workpiece can easily be sanded by hand to prepare the piece for surface treatment.

PROJECTS

Fig. 21

Fig. 22

Fig. 23

Fig. 24

Fig. 25

Fig. 26

NATURAL PLUM WOOD BOWL

Natural Applewood Bowl

This workpiece has only a limited connection with woodturning, but I would still like to present this technique, since it can be used to create wonderful pieces. This bowl was shaped using the properties of the wood. You could say that this piece almost made itself.

The Process

Using the bandsaw, cut a piece of green wood from the root system to a plate approximately $9/32"$ (7 mm) thick.

Presand it on both sides, using a handheld orbital sander. Place a bucket filled with water in a warm but shady place. In the winter months, you can do this in a well-heated workshop. Moisten the underside of the plate with water, using a brush. Then place the plate over the water bucket, with the damp side facing down. The upper side can now release the moisture into the ambient air, while the lower side remains moist due to the water in the bucket. The uneven drying of both sides causes the plate to warp into a bowl as the underside bends into the bucket. From time to time, the lower side can be repeatedly coated with water. Depending on the type of wood, moisture content, material thickness, and humidity, this process can take several hours. **(figs. 1–3)**

Fig. 1

Fig. 2

Fig. 3

Fig. 4

Fig. 5

Fig. 6

NATURAL APPLEWOOD BOWL

Once the surface of the bowl has dried, sand and surface-treat it by hand. **(fig. 4)**

A ring is turned as a bowl base, which is later fitted to the irregular outer contour. **(figs. 5–8)**

Place the ring on the underside of the bowl and center it. **(fig. 9)**

Use a pencil to draw a line along the top of the base that matches the curve of the bowl's underside. **(fig. 10)**

Shape the contour in small steps, using a grinding mandrel, which is mounted in the box column drill press. Repeated checking and reworking are essential to achieve a perfect fit. **(figs. 11–12)**

Once the ring has been fitted precisely, glue it to the underside of the bowl, using a two-part epoxy. **(fig. 13)**

This material has the added advantage of adhering easily to surface-treated material. Ask your local woodworking shop for a suitable adhesive material. Surface-treat the base first, followed by the entire shell on both sides. **(fig. 14)**

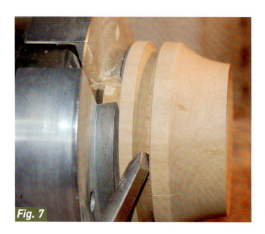
Fig. 7

Fig. 8

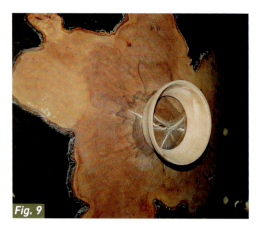
Fig. 9

Fig. 10

PROJECTS

Fig. 11

Fig. 12

Fig. 13

Fig. 14

NATURAL APPLEWOOD BOWL

Plate

The shape of a turned plate holds infinite possibility. It can be flat, deep, large, or small. The thickness of the wall can also be determined by the turner, who can then decide the level of difficulty of the workpiece. Your plate can be used as a functional item or a decorative object.

The Process

Screw a faceplate onto a circular green wood disk, which was cut out of a board with a bandsaw, and attach it to the lathe spindle. **(figs. 1-2)**

Once the correct speed has been set, you can start turning. Turn the disk round with the bowl gouge. Alternatively, you could use the large or medium gouge. To avoid tears, make sure that you do not turn beyond the edge. Remove small amounts of wood from both ends. **(figs. 3-4)**

Now the front face is turned flat. The turner starts at the stillest point, which is in the center of the turning axis. The gouge is set at an angle, turned slightly open, and guided to the outer edge, removing minimal wood at this stage. **(figs. 5-6)**

Use dividers to mark the base dimensions. **(fig. 7)**

Use the small gouge to turn the base, which is then used for clamping in the jaw chuck. **(figs. 8-9)**

Push the cutting edge slightly upward and turn the desired outer shape, which can be customized. **(figs. 10-12)**

Reclamp the workpiece so that the inner shape can be turned. **(fig. 13)**

Work the front face again. **(fig. 14)**

Remove shavings from the gouge to reduce material and turn the edge of the plate. **(figs. 15-17)**

Fig. 1

Fig. 2

Fig. 3

Fig. 4

Fig. 5

Fig. 6

PLATE

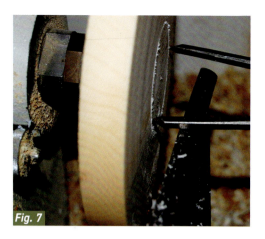
Fig. 7

Fig. 8

Fig. 9

Fig. 10

Fig. 11

Fig. 12

PROJECTS

Fig. 13

Fig. 14

Fig. 15

Fig. 16

Fig. 17

Fig. 18

PLATE

The thinner the material, the more the bowl tends to flutter or chatter. This unpleasant behavior creates an unattractive grid pattern on the inside of the bowl, making clean cuts a challenge. The fix for this lies in the turner's own hands. Support the back of the bowl with your fingers and press the gouge against the inside wall with your thumb. The edge of the bowl is now clamped between the hand and the gouge, avoiding unwanted fluttering. Pay particular attention to the sharp edge present on thin plates, since it could very easily cut your hand. **(figs. 18–19)**

The thinner the edge, the more patience and care required of the turner. To guarantee success, I suggest turning the first plates a little thicker. The level of difficulty can then be increased step by step. A light source will help you finesse the material thicknesses. **(fig. 20)**

Measure the edge thickness with a double compass in order to make it even. **(fig. 21)**

Fig. 19

Fig. 20

Fig. 21

Fig. 22

PROJECTS

The two compasses mirror each other; one is used to pinch the material so that the measurement can be read off the second. **(figs. 22–23)**

Remove chips in small, careful increments, always measuring and checking against the compass. **(figs. 24–25)**

The more advanced the work is, the more slowly and patiently it must be carried out, with a light source providing support. For finer work especially, make sure your tools are perfectly sharp. **(figs. 26–27)**

Once you are satisfied with the plate's shape, sand the surface. **(fig. 28)**

While being sanded, the edge is guided between the fingers and the sandpaper. **(fig. 29)**

Since the material thickness in this case is just under $1/32$" (1 mm)—that is, there is little material to work with, and the friction of the sanding material generates heat—the wood dries very quickly. Initially, only a small amount of sanding dust is produced, and the sandpaper sticks together due to the moisture in the wood.

Fig. 24

Fig. 23

Fig. 25

PLATE

After a few minutes, you'll notice that the plate can be sanded more easily, and the plate edge becomes increasingly thin. **(fig. 30)**

After a few hours, you may notice that the wood warps slightly as it dries. There will not be any dry cracks, however, because the tension in the wood can be released due to the low thickness.

Fig. 26

Fig. 27

Fig. 28

Fig. 29

Fig. 30

PROJECTS

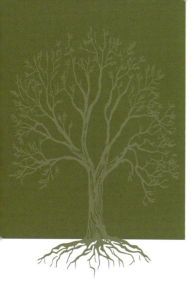

Sharpening Turning Tools

What Affects Sharpness?

Power Sharpening

Hand Sharpening

Every woodworker knows that starting with a good cutting edge is half the battle. After all, only really sharp tools help ensure enjoyable work and flawless results. A sharp cutting edge ensures that the fibers are cut off evenly and chips as fine as angel hair are removed, making the surface much smoother.

The work is more fun with a sharp edge!

This also greatly reduces the amount of sanding required, generating less dust and expending less excess material overall. In addition, fine cutting edges are more resistant to wear in the long term.

A poor cutting edge, on the other hand, is a nuisance, since it requires much more time and effort to work with. The quality of the workpiece also clearly suffers from poor cutting tools, since the fibers are not cut off but torn off, resulting in rough surfaces. **(figs. 1–2)**

What Affects Sharpness?

Good sharpness depends, among other things, on the steel's crystal structure. Basically, the finer the crystals in the material, the sharper the cutting edge. The shape of the tool or the cutting angle also influences the sharpness. Although blunt (more obtuse) angles do not achieve maximum sharpness, they last a long time in use. **(fig. 3)** Pointed (more acute) angles, on the other hand, become razor sharp but also tend to break off more easily and therefore become blunt more quickly. **(fig. 4)**

Last but not least, the possible sharpness also depends on the sharpening medium and the skill of the craftsman.

Power Sharpening

Before the actual sharpening, the **tools** must be **roughly prepared** on a bench grinder. This involves eliminating nicks by removing material. To avoid accidents and injuries, it is essential to wear safety glasses. **(fig. 1)** Ensure that the cutting edge does not become too hot during sharpening.

Fig. 1

Fig. 2

Generally speaking, the harder the steel, the more susceptible it is to high temperatures. Hardened steel should not be heated above 1,238°F (670°C). Overheating the steel is equivalent to tempering, as is necessary in steel production. This causes the alloy elements to burn partially or completely, rendering the steel unusable.

Due to the change in the microstructure of the steel, which can occur even before the steel glows blue, the crystals become larger and no longer hold together as well. The tool loses surface hardness, which in turn reduces its maximum possible sharpness. **(figs. 2–3)**

Good woodturners sharpen their tools freehand. The iron is held with the dominant hand, while the other hand rests on the bench grinder, with the thumb on the tool. **(fig. 4)**

Of course, there are also various sharpening devices for different tools that make sharpening easier.

It is also important to use suitable grinding wheels. Only the round grinding wheel, for example, produces the desired hollow grinding, which is essential for the turner. **(fig. 5)**

The hollow grinding ensures that the bevel slides along the workpiece and that the tool moves easily through the wood. Sanding is also made easier, since the entire surface does not have to be polished. The hollow grinding also prevents the bevel from balling up during sanding.

Fig. 3

Fig. 4

SHARPENING TURNING TOOLS

Fig. 5

Fig. 6

It is also important to choose the right whetstone. Grinding on a bench grinder always produces a burr on the cutting edge; the burr must then be removed before you use the tool. **(fig. 6)**

The cutting edge also becomes rough due to the coarse grain of the grinding wheel. On the one hand, the whetstone ensures that the burr is removed, and on the other, it makes the cutting edge sharp and smooth. A finer grind removes less material. There are several different whetstones (various natural or artificial stones) that are used either with water or oil. Water whetstones are generally rougher than oil whetstones. An oil stone must not be used with water and a water stone that has been used with oil is subsequently an oil stone. Woodturners mainly use oil stones, but these have the disadvantage of dirtying your fingers.

Turning tools are **mainly ground dry**, as the tool has a lot of mass and a relatively large amount of material has to be removed. Therefore, I recommend white corundum grinding wheels, which are ceramically bonded. The grain size is between 60 and 100. **(fig. 7)**

Grain size refers to the number of abrasive grains per square centimeter. Coarse grinding wheels have a low number for grain size and fine grinding wheels have a high number for grain size. A grinding wheel always rotates toward the tool so that the heat generated is directed toward the mass of steel. If the heat were directed toward the cutting edge, which is weaker, it would overheat immediately.

Fig. 7

Fig. 8

POWER SHARPENING

Fig. 9

Fig. 10

I recommend using bench grinders with two sanding discs: one for the straight tools and one for the rounded ones. **(fig. 8)**

This can significantly reduce wear on the wheels. When purchasing a bench grinder, make sure that it runs with spindle accuracy and is vibration-free. To ensure perfect running accuracy, the grinding wheels must fit perfectly on the arbor.

It is very important that grinding wheels are not cracked (check by using the sound test). They must continue to run smoothly, be clean, and always have a good grip. Over time, the grinding wheels stick together due to sharpening or they become uneven and are no longer flat. The wheels must therefore be regularly dressed. On the one hand, this makes them flat and removes the stuck abrasive grain to expose new, sharp grain. Dressing stones made of silicon carbide are used for ceramic or resin-bonded white corundum grinding wheels. Grinding rollers made from special grinding wheels can also be used. **(figs. 9–10)**

An **alternative** to **grinding wheels** is the **CBN sharpening wheel**. This wear-free grinding wheel is made of steel with fine CBN grain (cubic boron nitride) on the circumference and flanks.

The advantages of this abrasive are as follows:

1. CBN has a hardness of 5,600 kg per mm² and is therefore almost as hard as diamond (7,000 kg/mm²).
2. Manual grinding is absolutely safe.
3. It has unlimited durability (lifetime).
4. There is no "burning" (blueing) of the cutting edge.
5. It has smooth rotation (with a diameter of 7⁷⁄₈" or 200 mm, the maximum speed is 1,500 revolutions per minute).

The wear-free CBN sharpening wheel, shown here mounted on a lathe, can also be clamped on any bench grinder.

Sharpening Skew Chisels

Skew chisels usually have a wedge angle of between 25 and 30 degrees and are sharpened at an angle. The exact angle can vary depending on the type of use, so a fixed measurement is not mandatory. *Note: For safety's sake, make sure to use a tool rest when power sharpening.* When sharpening, place the iron on the grinding wheel with the bevel, ensuring that the cutting-edge line is always parallel to the axis of rotation of the bench grinder. **(fig. 1)**

Skew chisel.

Correct (left) and improper (right) cutting edge

Now it is important to guide the steel exactly along an imaginary line. The two bevels must have the same angle (i.e., be the same length). **(fig. 2)**

It is also important to ensure that the cutting-edge line is straight, or at most slightly curved. However, it must never be significantly curved. **(fig. 3)**

To achieve this, apply moderate pressure alternately at both ends of the cutting-edge line during sharpening. The turner also moves the tool evenly (i.e., without changing the angle), parallel to the axis of rotation of the wheel. **(fig. 4)**

Sharpening continues until the cutting edge is free of nicks and a small burr forms on the cutting-edge line. As previously mentioned, excessive heat development must be avoided at all costs.

POWER SHARPENING

It is therefore necessary to allow the tools to cool down several times. Under no circumstances should you cool them with water, however, since this would cool the material too quickly.

Sharpening Finishing Tools

Finishing tools are sharpened in a similar manner to chisels. Take care to ensure that the cutting line is exactly straight. The iron is also moved back and forth in the direction of the axis of rotation. **(fig. 1)**

Just as you care regularly for your turning tools, make sure to care regularly for your grinding wheel. Finishing tools can be rounded on one or both sides, which is why sharpening requires a lot of patience and skill. First, grind the tool on the straight side and then move on to the curves.

Remove material alternately from the curved and straight edges. Aim for fluid movements to ensure a clean, consistent bevel.

Sharpening Turning Gouges

Turning gouges can be sharped flat, round, or pointed. The basic rule is the larger the woodturning gouge, the flatter it should be sharpened (e.g., roughing gouges). With experience, you'll be able to sharpen these tools perfectly.

When sharpening turning gouges, take care to ensure a continuous surface along the bevel. If it has corners and edges, it cannot be used. **(fig. 1)**

First, place the gouge on the grinding wheel, with the bevel at a right angle to the axis of rotation. **(fig. 2)**

Then carefully turn the tool along the entire surface of the bevel. **(fig. 3)**

This must be done without deviation at the same height of the grinding wheel. It is also possible to obtain a sharper finish by using another technique. To do this, rotate the turning gouge and push it up slightly at the same time. Then return it to the imaginary line with the same movement.

This is how both sides of the gouge are alternately sharpened. **(figs. 4–8)**

This technique also requires a smooth, consistent, and automated work cycle to achieve the desired result. Each tool should always be sharpened symmetrically.

Finishing tool.

Fig. 1

Turning gouge.

SHARPENING TURNING TOOLS

For added safety, use a tool rest when power sharpening.

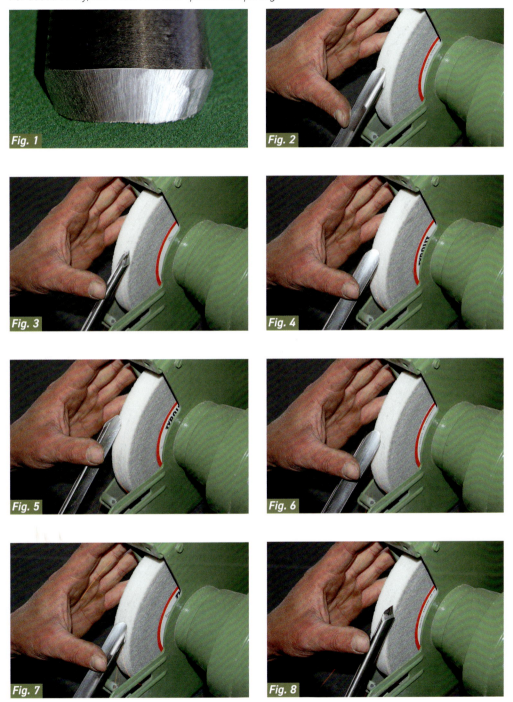

POWER SHARPENING

Hand Sharpening

Traditionally, woodturning tools are sharpened by hand. Flat whetstones are used for this purpose with the addition of oil or water. A basic distinction is made between natural stones, such as the Belgian Blue whetstone, Gosau whetstone, or Arkansas stone, and artificial stones. The latter are ceramically bonded and consist of corundum or silicon carbide. While artificial stones are available in a wide variety of grain sizes, the grain size of natural stones is often predetermined by nature and therefore unchangeable.

Various sharpening stones.

Belgian Blue

The Belgian Blue is one of the most famous whetstones for wet grinding. Some evidence suggests that it has been mined from the Belgian Ardennes since 1625. The Belgian Blue is a 480-million-year-old, grayish-yellow sedimentary rock made of volcanic ash, clay, and very fine garnets. This natural mixture and the extreme hardness of the garnets lends itself well to grinding hard metal tools. When using this stone, there is little or no burr, only a kind of polish on the surface of the tools, which ensures long-lasting sharpness. The gray version is another medium-quality variety. In 1996, a blue variety was discovered, which is slightly coarser than the yellow version.

Gosau Whetstone

This whetstone, which has been quarried since the thirteenth century, originated in the Austrian Salzkammergut region. It consists of bedrock that is bound with lime and chalk, and it comes in grain sizes ranging from 100 to 1,500. Due to its particularly sharp abrasive grain, this sandstone is very suitable for sharpening.

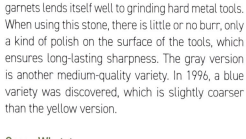

Belgian Blue.

Gosau whetstone.

Arkansas Stone
This whetstone is made of white or black quartzite and comes from Arkansas. The white quartzite is softer than the black quartzite. It has a grain size of 6,000 to 8,000 and is typically used with oil or petroleum. Thanks to its extreme hardness, it wears far more slowly than other natural stones.

Arkansas stone.

Sharpening
If the stone and cutting edge work well together, the stone will remain sharp and flat for a long time. This is the only way to ensure that the blunt grains break off and make way for new, sharper grains, which also ensures quicker material removal. When the whetstone takes on a black color, this is a sign that material has been removed. **(fig. 1)**

Before you move to the polishing step, the burr created by sharpening with the grinding wheel must first be broken away to make it really sharp.

The woodturner always starts work on the bevel of the tool and, unlike the carpenter, guides the stone over the iron. The easiest way to do this is to take the steel in the nondominant hand and support the tool handle on the forearm. **(fig. 2)**

With the whetstone in your dominant hand, you can begin to produce the cutting edge.

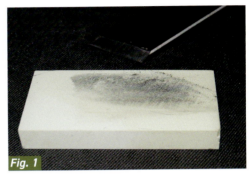

Correct (left) and incorrect (right).

HAND SHARPENING

The turner always starts with a coarse stone and works up to a fine stone. It is important that the stone always lies snugly against the bevel and is moved up and down evenly with moderate pressure. **(fig. 3)**

The bevel and mirror are then sanded alternately, causing the burr to bend back and forth. This also makes it thinner and thinner until it finally breaks off.

However, this process produces fine iron threads from the burr that remain on the stone. If you grind over these areas with the tool, the cutting edge becomes rough and blunt again. For this reason, the iron threads and iron splinters must always be consistently washed off.

During sharpening, the abraded whetstone also generates a kind of paste that produces a particularly fine grind or polish.

Since the stones become hollow over time during sharpening (especially with gouges), they must be sanded flat occasionally by using a coarse, flat sandpaper.

A disk or edge-grinding machine can also be used for this purpose. To minimize wear, every turner should also have several sharpening stones: one set for straight tools and the other set for rounded tools. Hollow chisel stones, for example, are best suited for sharpening gouges and rounded tools. **(figs. 4–6)**

For straight tools such as chisels and finishing tools, on the other hand, straight whetstones and combination whetstones are preferable.

Fig. 4

Fig. 5

Fig. 6

Surface Finishing

Stains

Varnishes

Oils and Waxes

For technical and aesthetic reasons, woodworkers usually apply a surface finish once a project is sanded. An appropriate surface finish can keep the wood from discoloring over time; in addition, finishes help protect against damage from dirt or humidity changes. Treated surfaces are also better protected against external chemical and physical effects such as cleaning agents, alcohol, and scratches. The structure and grain of the wood are emphasized to varying degrees by the different types of treatment. Surface finishes can also give wood a richer color and accentuate certain naturally occurring features, such as distinctive figuring or interesting knots.

An appropriate surface finish can prevent yellowing or graying of the wood.

Resin-rich woods should be treated with ammonia or alcohol prior to staining.

Woodturners use stains, varnishes, oils, and waxes primarily to seal the surface of their projects. Before a workpiece is finished, ensure that the wood surface has been sanded clean (120–240 grit). If necessary, wet the wood's surface before treatment, which will make it more receptive to the stain, as well as aiding in a more consistent color. Very resin-rich woods, such as pine or larch, should be deresinated with ammonia or alcohol before treatment. This enables even absorption of moisture and dye and successfully prevents resin from leaking through the surface material at a later stage. The surface treatment is carried out either directly on the lathe, with the workpiece rotating at low speed, or in an unclamped state. In both cases, you can apply your choice of finish by using a brush, cloth, or spray gun.

Stains

Stains change the color tone of wood surfaces and can therefore bring out the grain better. However, they do not seal the surface. When staining, make sure that the liquid is well stirred, to avoid any blotches. In addition, stains must always be applied when cold, with the excess stain being regularly wiped off. Since the end grain is more absorbent and therefore absorbs more stain, there may be uneven absorption and therefore color differences depending on the type of wood. To prevent this, soak the workpiece in water before staining. Prestaining with diluted stain also counteracts color differences. Stains usually dry gently at room temperature. The following types of stains are available:

- dye stains
- chemical stains
- pigmented stains

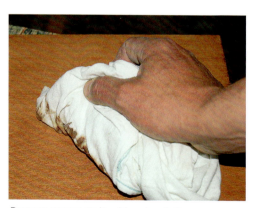

Remove excess stain with a dry cloth.

SURFACE FINISHING

Varnishes

A varnish completely seals the surface of a workpiece by forming a protective layer on it. The following varnish systems are available.

- nitro varnishes
- acid-curing coatings
- polyurethane varnishes
- synthetic resin coatings
- water-based varnishes

Apply varnish with a spray gun.

The choice of varnish depends on the use and location of the workpiece. Nitro varnishes, for example, should not be used outdoors, since they are not resistant to water and light.

Synthetic resin coatings and acid-curing coatings are usually much more resistant. It should be noted that polyurethane paints often consist of two components. This means that the paint to be applied must first be mixed in the correct ratio. The respective mixing ratio, viscosity, and shelf life can be found in the manufacturer's instructions.

There are also different gloss levels for varnishes—G10 to G100. Application is usually carried out with a spray gun. Often a fine intermediate sanding is essential between the application of the base coat and topcoat, to ensure that the topcoat adheres better.

Oils and Waxes

Over the years, great progress has been made in the development of wood-finishing products with oil and wax bases, so that alternatives to varnish are now available for many surfaces. Wood as a natural material goes well with oils and waxes, since the natural properties of the wood are largely retained when treated with these finishes. One advantage of oiled and waxed surfaces is that they are largely free of harmful substances, which can have a positive effect on people's health. The diffusion capacity and breathability of the wood are also hardly restricted by these products. This means that even a low residual moisture content in the wood is irrelevant.

Oils and waxes usually consist of several components. There are many different types of oils and waxes, including those listed below:

- Thistle oil is obtained from the seed of the thistle.
- Safflower oil is obtained from safflower seeds.
- Soybean oil comes from soybean seeds.
- Castor oil is obtained from the castor bean, the seed of the castor plant.
- Linseed (flaxseed) oil is obtained by pressing linseeds, one of the most widely used products on the market. However, it has the disadvantage of slow drying and yellowing on light-colored woods.

Different oils and waxes.

Make sure to sand a workpiece only if it is clean and free of dust and grease, moving up gradually from low-grit to high-grit sandpaper. Oils must be stirred carefully before use; you can apply them by using a spray gun, brush, cloth, or sponge. The surface material and the workpiece should be at room temperature, and excess must be wiped off. Depending on the absorbency of the wood,

- Carnauba wax is one of the hardest natural waxes. This vegetable wax is made from a palm-like plant.
- Candelilla wax is made from a cactus-like grass plant.
- Beeswax is derived from bees and has a pleasant aroma.
- Shellac wax is made from the excretions of the wax scale insect.
- Kerosene waxes are fossil waxes.

In principle, the same **principles** apply to each of these surface materials:

- Observe manufacturer's instructions and data sheets.
- Prepare a surface sample.
- Observe the processing temperature.
- Ensure that the wooden surfaces are cleanly prepared.
- Use clean tools.
- Observe the correct mixing ratio.
- Observe the correct viscosity.
- Practice caution with older materials.

Apply oil with a paintbrush.

Wipe off the excess.

apply two or three coats, allowing a drying time of approximately twelve hours after each coat. Drying times vary depending on the product; the exact drying time can be found in the individual data sheets. As a basic principle, it is better to dry a piece for more time than is needed, rather than not enough.

After coating, the oil or wax penetrates the uppermost layers of the wood and crystallizes after drying. This makes the surface highly resistant to all kinds of influences, such as moisture and dirt. Before recoating, sand the workpiece with sandpaper or a sanding fleece in order to smooth out the fibers raised by the moisture of the oil.

The grit of the abrasive should be 220 to 240. After the last coat has dried, polish the surface with a linen cloth.

Wash out the used tools with turpentine oil. Since oil- and wax-soaked cloths can spontaneously combust, take particular care with these surface materials. The soaked cloths must be disposed of in a closed metal container or hung up outside in an airy place.

Surface treatments of any kind can significantly enhance a workpiece. For this reason, make sure not to skimp on the time spent at this stage. A good woodturner will always treat a finished workpiece with care and effort, using the appropriate surface materials.

A workpiece finished by surface treatment.

| 155

OILS AND WAXES

Inspiration Gallery

by Sigmund Linortner,
Strobl am Wolfgangsee

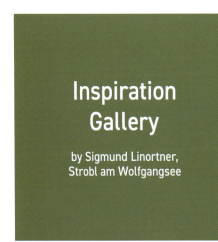

INSPIRATION GALLERY

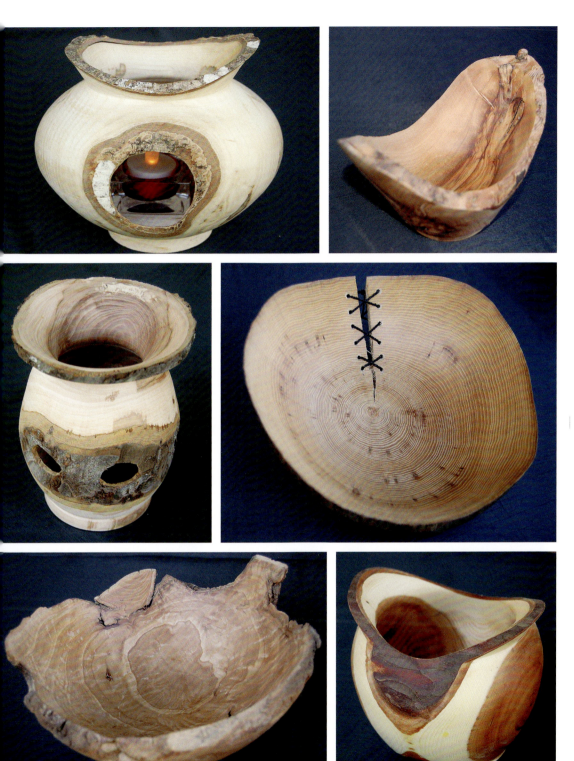

INSPIRATION GALLERY

Postscript

No master woodworker has ever fallen from the sky, and if they had, they wouldn't have survived. Learning manual skills requires a lot of patience and time. This skill can grow only through constant work and a variety of experiences. It may be that this learning process is made easier or shortened for some people due to natural talent, but the important thing is that they enjoy their work. A piece of work does not have to be perfect to be satisfying; rather, it is often the doing itself that contributes to achieving inner peace and relaxation.

With this book, I have tried to introduce woodturners to the many possibilities of turning green wood. If you don't succeed on the first attempt, I urge you to get up and try again. Through the amount of experience gained and the mistakes made, every project will eventually lead to success.

Finally, I would like to thank Martin Gschwandtner from the Austrian Federal Forests for his support. Special thanks go to Sigmund Linortner for the photo material provided.

Christian Zeppetzauer

Appendix

Glossary

bevel	Slanted edge
clamping	Fastening the workpiece to the lathe spindle
cutting-edge geometry	Angle ratios on a tool's cutting edge
darkening	Discoloration due to UV light
end face	End grain
end grain	Cut surface perpendicular to the fiber
face turning	Turning a flat surface at a right angle to the axis of rotation
finishing	Smoothing the wood surface after roughing
graying	Gray discoloration of the wood surface due to weathering
groove	Flat or semicircular channel-shaped recess
hazel spruce	Mountain spruce with narrow, folded annual rings
hollow grinding	Created by the rounding of the grinding wheel
honing	Refining the tool surface and removing the burr after sharpening
longitudinal timber	According to the grain orientation
ogee	S-shaped profile form
piercing	Production of recesses
pith	Central section of a standing trunk
planing	Creation of flat surfaces
roughing	Rough processing of the working surface
round rod	Turned shape with semicircular cross-section
sapwood	Light ring between bark and heartwood
tearing	Splintering of wood fibers
tool grip	Tool handle
turning on the fly	Turning without tailstock
turpentine oil	Alternative solvent or thinner, derived from pine trees
wedge angle	Cutting-edge angle, angle between mirror and bevel surface

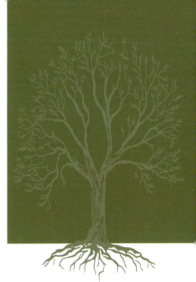

References

Klempe, K. 2001. *Wood Pests*. Berlin: Verlag Bauwesen.
Knuchel, H. 1995. *Wood Defects*. Hannover, Germany: Verlag Th. Schäfer.
Konig, F., G. Struber, and J. Hasenbichler. 1998. *Carpenter's Materials*. 5th ed. Vienna: Österreichischer Gewerbeverlag.

Additional Resources

Fa. Complex Farben Josef Schellhorn GmbH A-6334 Schwoich
Holzabsatzfonds D-53175 Bonn
Europa Lehrmittel
Christoph Richter

Note: Page numbers in *italics* indicate projects.

alder wood, 20
apple wood, 19, *128-31*
Arkansas stone whetstones, 149
asymmetrical trunks, hollows, 31

Ball, *95-106*
bark beetle, 45
Bark Bowl Variation, *115-21*
beech wood, 21, 29, 31, 32, 36, 38, 42, 82
beetle damage, 43-44, 45
Belgian Blue whetstones, 148
bowls
    Bark Bowl, *107-14*
    Bark Bowl Variation, *115-21*
    Natural Apple Wood Bowl, *128-31*
    Natural Plum Wood Bowl, *122-27*
boxwood, 19, 34-35
branches (branchiness), 36-38
    dead, 36, 37
    overgrown (green), 37
    rotten, 37
    wing, 37, 38
brown rot, 47
burls, 33-34

carpenter ants, 44-45
cherry wood, 20, *75-81*, *95-106*
chisels, sharpening. *See* sharpening turning tools
compression wood, 34-35
cracks, 38-39
crookedness, 27-28
cup, long-stemmed, *57-73*

definitions of terms, 159
discoloring fungi, 47
disease prevention, 46
diseases, wood, 46-47
dry cracks, 39
drying workpieces, 25. *See also* disease prevention

eccentric growth, 29-30
environment, wood characteristics and, 42

felling trees, 41-42
finishing surfaces, 151-55
    about: overview and general guidelines, 151-52
    oils and waxes for, 153-55
    stains for, 152
    varnishes for, 153
finishing tools, sharpening. *See* sharpening turning tools
Flower Vase, *74-81*
foreign objects, ingrown, 41
forked growth, 29
frost cracks, 39
fungi, wood-destroying, 47
furniture beetle, 44

gallery, for inspiration, 156-57
glossary of wood types, 18-22
Gosau whetstones, 148-49
gouges, sharpening. *See* sharpening turning tools
greater horntail, 44
green wood. *See also* wood
    drying workpieces, 25
    sourcing, 48-49
    storage options, 23-24
green woodturning
    about: overview of, 12-13; this book and, 10-11, 158
    conventional woodturning vs., 13
    possibilities with, 12-13
growth factors. *See* wood characteristics

hand sharpening, 148-50

heartwood. *See also specific wood species*
    abnormal formation (brown, pointed, red), 38
    characteristics of, 15-16, 18
    cracks, 39
    false, incomplete, 29, 36, 42
    rot, 47
heat cracks, 39
hornbeam, 22, 30
horntail, greater, 44

ingrown foreign objects, 41
insect damage, 43-45
Inspiration Gallery, 156-57

Lidded Vessel, *82-94*
longhorn beetle, 43-44
Long-Stemmed Cup, *57-73*

man-made damage, characteristics of, 40-42
maple wood, 18, 33, 42, 51, 57
moisture, storing green wood and, 23-24

Natural Apple Wood Bowl, *128-31*
Natural Plum Wood Bowl, *122-27*

oils and waxes, 153-55. *See also* finishing surfaces
olive wood, 21

pear wood, 19
pest damage, 43-45
Plate, *132-38*
plum wood, 22, *122-27*
power sharpening, 141-47
projects
    about: drying workpieces, 25; Inspiration Gallery and, 156-57; overview of, 50
    Ball, *95-106*
    Bark Bowl, *107-14*
    Bark Bowl Variation, *115-21*
    Flower Vase, *74-81*
    Lidded Vessel, *82-94*
    Long-Stemmed Cup, *57-73*
    Natural Apple Wood Bowl, *128-31*
    Natural Plum Wood Bowl, *122-27*
    Plate, *132-38*
    Small Turned Tree, *51-56*

reaction wood, 34-35
resin pockets, 36
ring shakes, 39
rings
    burls and, 33-34
    irregular growth ring structure, 32
    rippled growth, 32-33
rippled growth, 32-33
roots
    burls and, 33
    rot, 46-47
    strong growth of, 31
    tree crookedness and, 28
    wood growth and, 15
rot, types of, 46-47

sapwood, 15, 16, 18, 43, 47,sharpening turning tools, 140-50
    about: "good edge" importance, 140
    chisels, 145-46
    devices for, 143-44
    factors affecting sharpness, 141
    finishing tools, 146
    hand sharpening, 148-50
    hardness of steel and, 142, 143
    power sharpening, 141-47
    turning gouges, 146-47
shrinkage cracks, 38-39

shrinkage/swelling of wood, 16-18
Small Turned Tree, *51-56*
stains, 152. *See also* finishing surfaces
storing green wood, 23-24
structural factors of wood. *See* wood characteristics
Swiss stone pine, 22

tapering of a tree, 30
tension wood, 34-35
terms, definitions of, 159tree, small turned, *51-56*
trunk rot, 46-47
turkey tail rot, 47
turning gouges, sharpening. *See* sharpening turning tools
twisted growth, 35

varnishes, 153. *See also* finishing surfaces
vase, *74-81*
vessel, lidded, *82-94*

walnut wood, 21
water, storing green wood in, 23-24
waxes and oils, 153-55. *See also* finishing surfaces
whetstones, sharpening tools with, 148-50
white rot, 47
wildlife/insect damage, 43-45
wood. *See also* green woodturning; heartwood; *specific wood species*
    about: natural forests and, 9-10; this book and, 10-11
    bark, 15, 18
    bast tissue, 15, 45
    glossary of species/characteristics, 18-22
    green vs. dry, 13 (*See also* green wood)
    growth process affecting characteristics, 14-16
    sapwood, 15, 16, 18, 43, 47shrinkage and swelling, 16-18
    woodturning possibilities, 14
wood characteristics
    about: overview of, 26-27
    abnormal heartwood, 38
    asymmetrical trunks, hollows, 31
    branchiness, 36-38
    burls, 33-34
    compression wood, 34-35
    cracks, 38-39
    crookedness, 27-28
    eccentric growth, 29-30
    environmental factors, 42
    external influences affecting, 38-47
    felling trees causing, 41-42
    forked growth, 29
    fungi and, 46-47
    growth factors, 27-31
    ingrown foreign objects, 41
    irregular growth ring structure, 32
    man-made damage, 40-42
    reaction wood, 34-35
    resin pockets, 36
    ring shakes, 39
    rippled growth, 32-33
    strong root growth, 31
    structural factors, 32-38
    tension wood, 34-35
    transport damage, 42
    tree taper, 30
    twisted growth, 35
    wildlife/insect damage, 43-45
    wood diseases and, 46-47
wood-destroying fungi, 47

yew wood, 20, 30, 31

Celebrate the Natural Elegance of Green Wood

Get to know the age-old craft of green wood turning with expert tips, interesting techniques, and over 500 photos.

Step by step, the author guides you through the creation of ten unique projects, as well as two fascinating techniques for bending green wood. The workpieces include decorative balls, small turned trees, rustic bowls with bark edges, elegant plates, and more.

Tips on choosing the right materials, storing wood, troubleshooting challenges, and drying finished pieces makes it easier to dive into the craft. Advice on surface treatment and proper sharpening ensures that your finished creations are a sight to behold. Newcomers to the art form can start their turning journey here, while advanced woodworkers will find useful techniques to grow their skills with confidence.

CONTAINS

- detailed techniques for woodturning with green wood;
- selection, drying, finishing, and tool sharpening;
- a glossary of preferred woods;
- ten projects: vases, balls, bowls, plates, and more.